Classic
Diners of
MAINE

SARAH WALKER CARON

AMERICAN PALATE

Published by American Palate
A Division of The History Press
Charleston, SC
www.historypress.com

All photos by Sarah Walker Caron.

First published 2020

Manufactured in the United States

ISBN 9781467141031

Library of Congress Control Number: 2020930488

This book is dedicated to diner lovers everywhere.

And to my two kids, Will and Paige. Always.

Contents

Preface

I t's a cold March day the first time I pull into the parking lot of the Miss Portland Diner on Marginal Way. Snow covers the ground and bare tree branches frame the scene in the late afternoon sun. Inside, we head to the dining car—one of two dining spaces inside the renovated, decades-old diner. It's decorated with shiny green shamrocks and all of the waitresses are wearing green Miss Portland Diner shirts. The specials on this cold, winter St. Patrick's Day are all, appropriately, Irish themed. Or, at least, American Irish themed.

The space is like stepping back in time—a well-preserved glimpse into American diner history.

We order green milkshakes to sip. They're made with Gifford's vanilla ice cream, milk and green sprinkles, which change the color when swirled. It's vanilla flavored, though I would have loved for it to be minty.

I order the signature corned beef hash and eggs, and the waitress compliments my choice. It's her favorite, she tells me, and she eats it daily with rye toast. It seems I've chosen well.

She chats with us about the locally made confections the diner serves. Cakes are brought in regularly. They are kept on the counter on covered cake plates—so tempting. The whole interaction is pleasant, fun, welcoming. Isn't that how a diner should be?

When the hash comes, the rich, caramel-colored outside looks mouthwateringly good. It's been fried to a crisp, just how I like it. But as I dig in, I realize this house-made corned beef hash is nothing like the canned stuff I expected. No, it's better, way better.

The Miss Portland Diner from the outside on March 17, 2018.

Shredded corned beef, so-tender carrot and potato pieces and caramelized onions combine to make this a sophisticated alternative to the traditional. I love it. The perfectly cooked eggs with creamy, runny yolks complement the tangy corned beef. The rye toast is toasted to a just-right light brown and lightly buttered. Afterward, I order a cup of the smooth coffee, adding cream and sugar. I sip it, savoring the warmth and the experience.

The Miss Portland Diner was the first stop on my journey visiting diners through Maine, interviewing owners and writing this book.

On a cold, snowy January day, I made my last stop. It's a long drive from Bangor to Rumford where the charming, quirky, friendly Deluxe Diner has stood since it opened in 1928. We park on the street, hopeful that we are actually in a parking space. (It's hard to tell with all that snow.)

From the outside, this small building looks like a tiny brick and clapboard one that's survived Rumford growing around it. But as you step to the heavy, wooden sliding entrance door, you can see inside to the pristine interior of a Worcester Lunch Car Company dining car.

At first, it seems we won't find a place to sit and will just have to stand awkwardly until someone finishes eating. It's counter seating only in this classic that is owned by a pair of sisters who dole out a side of sass and laughter with every order. But customers kindly scooch over, giving us two stools together at the counter.

Above: Green milkshakes were on special on St. Patrick's Day 2018 at the Miss Portland Diner.

Right: The house-made corned beef hash at the Miss Portland Diner, shown with rye toast and eggs over easy.

The Deluxe Diner is located in Rumford, Maine.

It's tight in here, built for a time when Americans were smaller. But we settle in, coats hung on the coat tree in the corner, and take in the gleaming stainless steel and friendly atmosphere.

We order. Coffee. Corned beef hash. Eggs. Toast. Blueberry pancakes. Bacon. One of the sisters chides us for not ordering their signature hash browns ("Best around!" she tells us), so we add an order of those too.

The diner, which closes at noon, stops seating at about 11:30 a.m. We are the last ones seated. Other folks, hoping for the familiar comforting fare, are turned away at the door. We end up being the last diners eating that day and strike up a conversation with the sisters about how they got to Rumford and came to own the diner. I can't wait to interview them later in the week.

As I reflected on the experience later, I smiled knowing my tour of Maine diners started and ended with Worcester Lunch Car Company dining cars. They are my favorite.

Research for this book took me all over Maine through the end of one winter into spring, summer, fall and the beginning of another winter. What a journey. Along the way, I ate a lot of corned beef hash (you'll notice almost every diner in this book has a description of its corned beef offering);

talked to a lot of waitstaff, owners and historical societies; read countless old newspaper stories; and spent hours identifying the right diners to include. I spent even more hours trying to pinpoint the histories of the diners using historical society records, newspaper clippings and interviews.

This book wouldn't have been possible without the generosity of folks around the state who answered my countless questions about diners and diner histories. It also wouldn't have been possible without the diners themselves. To them, I am eternally grateful.

WHAT IS A DINER?

Before I could begin working on this book, I had to decide on an important quandary: What makes a diner a diner?

For some, this is an obvious question. A true diner can only be so if it's housed in a dining car or other diner building—something made especially for a diner. And once upon a time, that was true across the board. Companies like Worcester Lunch Car Company, Fodero Dining Car Company and Bixler Manufacturing Company were manufacturing diners in a variety of styles through much of the early to mid-twentieth century.

But things change and so do our definitions of what makes a diner a diner. See, if I were to stick to that purist definition, it would discount many of Maine's most beloved diners. Moody's, Becky's, the Maine Diner, the Brunswick Diner—none of these are actually dining car diners. But they are diners that have served hungry locals and motorists for decades. Moody's and Becky's were built on-site and expanded later. The Maine Diner was also built on-site. The Brunswick Diner was built by hand in Norway, Maine, where it operated as the Norway Diner early in its history.

So, I was willing to overlook the building if a diner had other compelling features that made it noteworthy as a classic. But there had to be a line somewhere.

Today, Maine, the Pine Tree State, has more than eighty eateries that call themselves, or otherwise self-classify as, "diners." These stretch from border to border and are housed in strip malls, converted houses, dedicated restaurant spaces, dining cars and more. There are other restaurants that call themselves family restaurants or cafés and share some of the characteristics of the classic diner. But family restaurants are a different breed and so are cafés. And there are some that fall most squarely into the dive category—

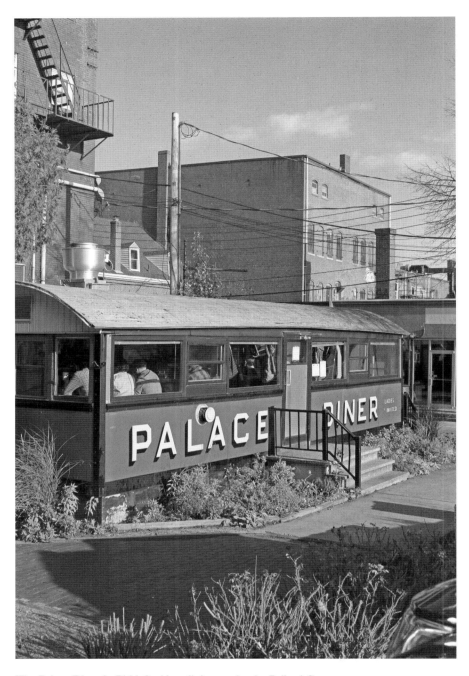

The Palace Diner in Biddeford is a dining car by the Pollard Company.

A Palais Royale and Fries is waiting to be eaten as a waiter works behind the counter at the Palace Diner in Biddeford.

something that has gotten more notoriety and popularity in the wake of Guy Fieri's popular show *Diners, Drive-Ins and Dives*.

To narrow my list, I only considered establishments that self-identify as diners. Dysart's in Hermon, for instance, is a beloved eatery, but it considers itself a restaurant and truck stop. Plus, given the size, it didn't quite fit the criteria for this list. However, eateries that are housed in dining cars were all included. As were a few hand-built diners, ones built up from lunch carts and a beloved one that Stephen King has eaten at many times in the Queen City.

Here's the basic criteria I used to narrow my list:

- A diner usually has an all-day breakfast menu
- A diner has counter seating, usually
- A diner has a kitchen behind the counter, usually
- A diner is usually a smaller, stand-alone restaurant

You'll notice there's a lot of "usually" in that list. There are no absolutes. As I visited diners, I realized that for each rule I came up with, there was an exception. And again, I am not a purist. Others will disagree with me, but I don't believe a diner has to be in a Pollard or Worcester or Mountain View or any other prefabricated building.

There are so many more establishments that call themselves diners and fit some of these criteria. This book isn't intended to be an exhaustive look at diners in Maine. It's a history of some classic diners (and a few modern classics) worth considering as you seek a place for the perfect hash browns or the best omelet.

Maine is home to so many great diners. This book highlights ones that have become cultural icons in the Pine Tree State. For each of the ones mentioned, I can recount a conversation or social media posting of a friend extolling the virtues of the given diner. "That's where we always stopped on vacation!" "Whenever we return from a road trip, that's a must-stop for us." "That's the best diner in Maine."

So many memories surround these diners. So many stories can be told of stops there and meals consumed. And is it any wonder? Diners are a hallmark of American life. They are places where families have stopped for decades.

Do you remember your first diner? One of my first diner memories comes from 1987 in Wappingers Falls, New York. It was October and an unseasonable blizzard had just swept through the area where we lived. Left without power for days, there was no school, no heat and no hot meals at home. The Imperial Diner on Route 9 was a refuge for my grandmother and me. Warm and toasty with mugs of hot cocoa and marshmallows, the diner was a salve on the uncertainty of those strange days. It provided a warm meal, comfort food, a little peace.

There were others too. Ones stopped at on road trips or late at night after play rehearsals. And there were the ones that provided a familiar menu in a comfortable place in times of great stress.

When I moved to Maine, Nicky's Cruisin' Diner was a familiar and easy place for my kids and me to find a good meal after challenging days getting settled into our new home. And Becky's Diner has been a favorite that I've taken friends to since first trying it not long after I arrived here.

Diners are part of my life, part of my history and now part of my writing repertoire. I am so excited to share the stories of classic Maine diners from the late 1920s, when they first emerged, to today. As you leaf through the pages, I hope you discover something new and find stories that intrigue you. And I hope you'll be inspired to visit some of the diners in this book to see for yourself what makes them special.

But then again, diners are all special, aren't they? Between stacks of pancakes with melting lumps of butter and sandwiches piled with thick slices of house-roasted turkey, there's some magic to diners. They are the places we gather with friends after high school plays and football games. They are the places we meet up when we have a little spare time. And they're the places we take our kids for breakfast just because. Diners are woven into the fabric of our lives.

Acknowledgements

This book wouldn't have been possible without the time, patience and stomachs of my children, Will and Paige, and my significant other, Gibran Graham. Thank you all for visiting so many diners with me, sometimes in the same day, and letting me help you decide what to order. ("OK, who's having the corned beef this time?")

Thank you to Sue Denison and Charles Longley of the Norway Historical Society for helping me uncover the origins of the Norway Diner (now the Brunswick Diner). And thank you to Catherine Cyr, the museum services manager for the Pejepscot Historical Society in Brunswick for helping me follow the trail farther. Without the help of these three people, I wouldn't have uncovered the true history of this classic diner. Who knew there were two Miss Brunswick Diners that had operated in Brunswick?

Thank you to Louise Merriman and Charles Butler from the Biddeford Historical Society for your assistance in clearing up the timeline of the Palace Diner.

A warm thank you to Druscilla Breton, archivist at the Rumford Historical Society, for your most needed help discovering the history of the Deluxe Diner. This diner that has stood in the same place in Rumford since 1928 hasn't received the same attention as similar diners in Maine but should.

Thank you also to all of the diner owners quoted in this book for helping me put together these histories. Your time and insights were invaluable. I am so happy to have heard from so many of you about what makes a diner a diner.

To all the waiters and waitresses who've served us over the last year at diners throughout Maine, thank you. You helped me realize that one of the key parts to a diner is the friendly atmosphere cultivated by you.

Thank you to my parents and siblings, Sue, Rick, Zach and Haley, for your continued support of my writing projects—and for not calling me crazy when I decided it was totally doable to write three books in a year while working four jobs and caring for my two kids.

And finally, thank you to my editor Michael Kinsella at Arcadia Publishing and The History Press for bringing the idea for this book to me. It's been an amazing journey researching and writing it, and I am so grateful to have had the opportunity to do so.

The Cultural Significance of Diners

It's near the clock tower—the literal center of life in Storybrooke, Maine. And there, inside the house that holds Granny's Diner, locals meet for coffee, drop in for breakfast or take out, celebrate birthdays and mourn bad news. This hub of activity is where new folks are told to go to find a helping hand and a friendly place. It's also where so many of the residents of Storybrooke begin their days.

Granny's Diner is, truly, a welcoming center of activity. And while Storybrooke is fictional (you might recall it from the *Once Upon a Time* television show that aired on ABC), the significance of diners to local life is not. This could have easily been written about diners in towns across Maine that serve as cultural hubs.

Diners in Maine are familiar places, serving familiar menus and welcoming folks from all over. Since the 1930s, Moody's Diner—a long, white building on a busy midcoast road—has been serving classic diner fare from its Waldoboro location. Today, it's run by the same family who opened it so many decades ago.

In Biddeford, the familiar red-and-black dining car Palace Diner has served hungry folks since being delivered by the Pollard Company of Lowell, Massachusetts, in 1927. Sure, those faces, and their stories, have changed over time—gone are the days of millworkers seated at the counter for a quick, cheap, good breakfast. And here are the days of this little diner, which still has "Ladies Invited" emblazoned on the outside, being written up by top publications as a must-try restaurant.

Moody's Diner has been on Route 1 in Waldoboro since the 1930s.

At the cozy Deluxe Diner in Rumford, perhaps Maine's best-kept diner secret, folks have been sliding open the diner door since the 1920s. With sixteen stools at the counter, alternatively covered with red and brown leather, the space is tight, but it works. These days, the sisters who run it have great rapport with each other and customers, greeting many of them by name and saying goodbye with things like "See you Wednesday!"

Diners are where families stop for breakfast before soccer games. It's where others drop in to celebrate a success. It's also where old friends gather for coffee in the early morning hours. And as folks travel up Interstate 95 or across the shoreline, it's where they stop for a bite along the way. Diners today draw locals and visitors alike.

Jane Davis, owner of the Brunswick Diner located on a section of Route 1 known as Pleasant Street, knows this well. Although her diner attracts a lot of tourists, particularly in the summer, it's the cast of regulars who have become an integral part of the diner family.

"Some regulars come in two times a day," Davis said. "It's kind of like home for them. They eat their meals there and then meet their friends there."

Davis's diner, which has been open since the late 1940s, has been a part of morning routines for decades. It's where young men gathered before work for a cup of coffee and conversation. And it's where they still gather now, even though they are retired, for the same thing.

"All these men, they come every morning, and they catch up with each other," Davis said of her so-called "6 a.m. crowd."

From prework catching up to postretirement socializing, the Brunswick Diner has been a part of their lives for decades. "We had a guest who came in the other day, he's in his nineties, who said he's been coming there since it opened," Davis said.

Across Maine, iconic diners come in all shapes and sizes. There are dining cars, little house-like structures, storefronts and corner diners. They have porcelain exteriors, brick, clapboard and more. But it's not what's outside that really matters. It's what's inside the diners—friendliness, familiarity, kindness.

Jim MacNeill, owner of the Maine Diner, recalls a time when he was on a motorcycle trip and dropped into the Agawam Diner, a cash-only classic dining car located in Rowley, Massachusetts.

"I'd never been. I was by myself. There was a counter seat open. I sat down, I ordered breakfast and I just started shooting the shit with the waitress— she'd been to [the] Maine Diner a bunch of times," MacNeill recalled.

After his breakfast and conversation, he wasn't done. MacNeill lingered, ultimately ordered lunch too and stayed a little longer. "That's not something that happens when you go to any other restaurant. There's a friendliness and there's a vibe and an energy that you just don't find in too many places," MacNeill said.

After his meals, he realized he didn't have cash. But the guy behind the register looked him over and said, "Yeah, I think I can trust you," allowing him to run to a nearby bank and come back to pay.

"It's friendly and down-to-earth," MacNeill said. The friendly atmosphere is welcoming to all. That, diner owners say, is part of what really makes a diner a diner.

Chad Conley, co-owner of the Palace Diner, recalls a mural that was behind the counter at the now-closed Big Mama's Diner in the Old Port neighborhood of Portland. He says it really captured this idea. It depicted a bunch of people from all walks of life sitting shoulder to shoulder at a diner counter enjoying a meal.

"[There's] a sense that all are welcome, the food is broadly appealing and it's a place that all elements of the community should feel welcome to come in and interact," Conley said.

Plus, there is the food. It's wholesome and simple. It's familiar. It's food that's been served in diners for decades. From the fluffy pancakes as big as

Behind the counter at the Palace Diner in Biddeford.

a plate to piles of perfectly crisped corned beef hash, diners serve familiar, classic comfort food to hungry patrons—some for generations.

"[There's] a certain sort of American cuisine that needs to be in place," said Conley. Diner food, as it's become known, is its own cuisine category.

"In the foodie era, we try to give you a place where you can come in and just have some meat and potatoes," said Dan Beck, president of Moody's Diner in Waldoboro. "In a rapidly changing world, we try to keep some things the same. We try to give you a place where you can slow down and recognize a familiar face."

And in a place where mac and cheese has been a Monday special for decades, that's important. Moody's, despite modernizing its ordering system and now accepting credit cards, has many employees who have worked there for years. And it has even—to appease customers, Beck said—held onto "the same straight-back, uncomfortable booths that we've had for decades [and] the same yellow laminate countertop that we've had for decades."

From the waitstaff to the cooks to the customers, there's a certain dynamic in diners. It's a feeling, a familiarity, a comfort level. MacNeill, sums it up in a single word: "energy."

"And the reason I say that is there's just a vibe to diners. When you go sit down at the counter and you've never been there, there's just a friendliness and just a vibe that you don't get in most restaurants," MacNeill said. "The energy comes from the lighting, the loudness, all of the things that don't happen at a stuffy fancy restaurant, and to me, that's comforting."

And perhaps there's a little more too. At the Deluxe Diner, a 1928 Worcester dining car set in the small western Maine mill town of Rumford, co-owner Jodi Campbell said there's a familiarity that quickly develops between the diner staff and the folks who come in. She and her sister, while running the diner, also interact with customers, "just chatting people up."

"The next time they come in you call them by name," Campbell said. Maybe that, in the end, is really what a diner is: a place where everyone is welcome.

1
The Early Days

Once a manufacturing capital, Maine was home to many textile and paper mills. Farm girls from around New England flocked to Biddeford and Saco where textile mills offered good wages and nearby housing in boardinghouses. Later, immigrants came and became employed in those mills too. Elsewhere—Rumford, Westbrook and Skowhegan, for instance—paper mills employed thousands. And as the second decade of the twentieth century set in, those workers were in need of good, inexpensive food at odd hours—early morning and late at night. So began a new industry of diners in Maine's busiest mill cities.

But it wasn't just millworkers who needed to eat. Visitors to Maine did too.

PALACE DINER—MAINE'S OLDEST DINER (1927)

18 Franklin Street, Biddeford
www.palacedinerme.com

Just off Main Street in the former mill town of Biddeford, Maine, sits a time capsule of a diner. For more than ninety years, the neat red-and-black dining car with a barrel roof, and which only seats fifteen, has stood on Franklin Street. Worn but clean Formica countertops hold plates of beautifully presented diner food. It's simple fare—burgers and fried chicken sandwiches

The Palace Diner shown from the outside.

for lunch and eggs and flapjacks or corned beef hash for breakfast—but it's done well and with panache.

Over the years, the Palace Diner has been carefully maintained by its owners (there have been seven so far). And, aside from the addition of an exterior kitchen in the 1980s, it's nearly identical to how it was when it arrived on Franklin Street in the 1920s. The Palace Diner, now owned and operated by business partners Chad Conley and Greg Mitchell, is the oldest diner still operating in Maine.

Its history began in 1926 in Lowell, Massachusetts, where the dining car was built by the Pollard Company, which only built a handful of dining car–style diners in 1926 and 1927, according to Charles Butler of the Biddeford Historical Society.

"Diners were at first converted old trolley and railroad cars. Then they were manufactured and sold as prefab units. The Palace Dinner is one of those manufactured units and not an old railroad car," Butler said.

Fresh from the assembly line, it was taken north to Biddeford and installed. The first owners, Louis Lachance of Kennebunk and his brother-in-law Orville Pollard (who, yes, was of the family who owned the company that built the dining car), opened the diner in 1927, at a time when the mills were booming and there was a great breakfast market to tap into.

"Biddeford had need of several cheap places to eat, places like the Nut Shell—the name describes it all," Butler said. "The mills flooded the streets at noon and shift changes with folks that had only an hour to find something to eat or were ravenous after a completed shift and wanted to eat before the journey home." The Palace Diner filled that need and became an essential part of Biddeford's thriving downtown.

In 1962, Lachance sold the diner to its second owner, Roland Beaudoin, who operated the dining car for a few years until his son, Raynald "Pete" Beaudoin, took over in the mid-1960s. News reports put the transition date sometime between 1964 and 1966.

At some point over the years, the dining car was moved from one end of the parking lot to the other. "Franklin Street is now mostly a parking lot. But it was one of the first areas of downtown Biddeford to develop," Butler said. Initially, the Palace Diner was located on the site of an old boardinghouse that had been torn down on the northern side of Franklin Street.

Later, when the city wanted to build a municipal parking lot, the Palace Diner was in the middle of the proposed parking lot, Butler said, but "the city thought to save it and moved it to the rear of the J.C. Penney building."

Aside from that move, the diner has basically been in the same spot for more than nine decades. In the 1980s, a kitchen addition was completed by Pete Beaudoin, who was behind the counter for about thirty years before retiring on June 28, 1996.

A plan long in the making, Pete Beaudoin had sought to find someone to run the diner after him. It continued to thrive as a beloved Biddeford eatery. Just before his planned retirement date, Pete Beaudoin reached an agreement with Tony Ouellette, who ran a competing breakfast spot nearby on Main Street. Ouellette was to lease and run the diner with the option to buy. However, that deal fell apart, and just six weeks later, the diner closed.

"Things didn't work out," Pete Beaudoin told the *Portland Press Herald* in September 1996.

Lease negotiations had fallen through, and a friend told the newspaper that Ouellette just wasn't ready to buy it. Others had a different take on the situation.

"Pete had his style and then Tony took over, and a lot of people didn't like it," Roger Fournell, a regular and a lieutenant with the Biddeford Fire Department, told the *Portland Press Herald* in September 1996.

The diner remained closed for more than a year, until Rick Bernier and his wife, Joanne, purchased it and reopening it in October 1997. "This is just what I wanted—a real, authentic diner," Bernier told the *Portland Press*

Herald in 1997. "There aren't a lot left in the country, so I'm fortunate that this was available."

On reopening day in October 1997, customers came back happy to have the landmark open again.

In November 2002, five years later, Bernier told the *Portland Press Herald* that he still loved the diner and all its shining stainless steel. "I'm here at quarter of 4 every morning like clockwork," Bernier said while plating food.

A few years later, though, it was time to sell. "I put a lot into this. It's an emotional thing," Bernier told the *Portland Press Herald* in October 2005.

In 2005, the Berniers sold the diner to Kyle Quinn of Biddeford and his wife, Debbie. Like Bernier, Quinn was thrilled to own the historic diner. He and his wife had wanted a restaurant, and when they learned that the Palace Diner was for sale, they had to have it. Quinn vowed to keep the menu and diner the same, with a few additions to the menu. "It's going to remain Biddeford's baby," Quinn said.

Quinn, who hadn't worked in restaurants before, found there was a steep learning curve when it came to running a diner. A few years later, in 2008, the Quinns listed the diner for sale. At the time, he told the *Portland Press Herald*, "I know it sounds absurd, but it's true: this is my baby. If it doesn't sell then—guess what?—I'm happy."

Three years later, in May 2011, it did sell. Quinn, for his part, continued running the diner until May 12, 2011. The new owners, the Capotosto family—David and his wife, Carmel, and their children, Nicholas, Paulina DeCastro, Jonathan, Samuel, Benjamin and son-in-law Vinicius DeCastro—reopened it several weeks later with a newly updated kitchen. Like their predecessor, they kept the menu very similar.

"We really love good breakfast," David Capotosto told the *Boston Globe* in March 2013. "So, we use cage-free eggs, and no cans were harmed in the making of our gravy."

Later that year, on August 31, the diner closed again. In November 2013, current owners Conley and Mitchell signed a lease on the place with the option to purchase. Conley said that he and Mitchell had been looking for a place to open a dive bar in Portland, but they'd had no luck. They had, coincidentally, already created an LLC to use for their business plan and banking. It was a name they thought would be good for their dive bar concept but, as it turned out, was more like serendipity for where they ended up. It was named Palace LLC before they even heard about or considered the Palace Diner.

"We just thought it was a cool name. We liked it. It fit the concept that we originally wanted to do," Conley explained. Then they heard that the Palace Diner was available and decided to check it out.

In the summer of 2018, they exercised their option, and purchased the diner they'd run for about four years. These days, there's sometimes a line for the Palace Diner's coveted fifteen seats. That happens more often in the summer and on Monday holidays. But the staff offers coffee to those who are waiting and on days with particularly bad weather, lets folks wait inside. But it's standing room only.

"We're so limited in terms of seats, so we kind of have to be unapologetic about that," Conley said. "We try to make people as comfortable as we can….There's only so much you can do, but we try to do what we can."

The popular diner that once drew crowds from the nearby mills now draws folks from near and far. Some come for the reliable food. Others come because the Palace Diner has been named in list after list of must-try eateries. In 2016, it was named the best diner in Maine in the Best of Maine reader's poll by *Down East* magazine. In 2017, writer Amy Traverso said in *Yankee* magazine that the Palace Diner has "the greatest tuna melt in lunch counter history." Eater.com named the diner one of its 38 Essential Restaurants in 2018, calling it "the ideal realization of a daytime Americana diner."

It was mentioned as a reason to drive eighteen miles south in acclaimed food magazine *Bon Appétit*'s naming of Portland, Maine, as the restaurant city of the year. Restaurant editor Andrew Knowlton wrote, "The flapjacks are towering, the burger is smashed and crunchy, and the tuna salad sandwich is quickly becoming a Maine icon."

The diner even was shortlisted for a coveted James Beard Award. In 2020, Mitchell and Conley were named semifinalists for the Best Chef–Northeast award. The best chef awards are judged by the region.

The recognition comes with good reason. The Palace Diner's limited menu was created that way by design—partially due to limited kitchen and seating space, but that's not all. "We want people, whatever they land on, we want it to be exceptional," Conley said. The scope of the menu allows them to focus on the details. "We try to sort of start the process of people liking our food by making it look good."

There are eight selections for breakfast and four sandwiches on the lunch menu, along with a few à la carte side options (most of which appear in part on other menu items). "Conceptually, the food is just normal, plain diner food. We're not adding red pepper jelly. We're just offering straightforward food," Conley said.

The lumberjack breakfast at the Palace Diner in Biddeford.

Highlights of the menu include the burly lumberjack breakfast, which includes sausage, bacon, flapjacks and eggs; the corned beef hash, served with two eggs and toast; and the Palais Royale and fries, a massive burger. Conley's favorite is the fried chicken sandwich, a juicy, perfectly breaded chicken breast served on a roll with cheese and more. "It's one of those things where when one person orders it and other people see it, we all of a sudden have a bunch of orders for it," Conley said.

Running such a small diner—the building is about 630 square feet, according to Zillow, and it sits on a lot that's about 871 square feet—is different than the places where Conley and Mitchell worked before.

"In some ways, it's easier because it's so limited. You're only dealing with fifteen customers at a time and five hundred square feet of the restaurant,"

The fried chicken sandwich at the Palace Diner in Biddeford.

Conley said. But in other ways, he said, it's more limited. "We really just don't have any more spare cubic inches of space. It sort of forces us to be creative with our space."

Ultimately, the space is among the things that make the Palace Diner unique. "Every restaurant is unique and has its own set of weird, unique things. Size for us is definitely that big obvious thing that makes us different. I think it forces us to be better. There's no wasted space. Everything has a purpose," Conley said.

Mitchell and Conley plan to keep the diner classic and the menu the same. It's been basically the same since they opened the diner, and though they'll occasionally change something small, they believe in consistency. "It's really important to us that the Palace Diner food is the Palace Diner food and it doesn't change much," Conley said. "We want to be able to live up to that dream [of a meal they've had]. We want people to be able to trust that recommendation they give."

And those people are the highlight of their tenure at the helm of the Palace Diner, Conley said. First, there's the staff, which has grown from just Conley and Mitchell and two employees to a team of ten, including themselves. "Several employees have been with us since the beginning," Conley said. Better yet, they've seen employees put down roots in Biddeford and buy homes. They've also seen an increase in folks from the town applying to work there. And they've hired some.

There are also the familiar faces of regulars. Conley, who works in the kitchen, says he doesn't see them as much as Mitchell, who is the face of the business, but there are some he makes a point to say hello to. "There are people who have been coming several times a week for years," Conley said. "It's really nice. I think any diner, any place, where it's affordably priced and the food is good—any place like that is going to have regulars."

And in addition to the local regulars (some of whom don't eat there during tourist season), there are also the summer regulars. "That's one of the markers of the summer season—we see people we haven't seen since the previous year," Conley laughed.

As Conley and Mitchell look to the future, they are planning some updates to the building, including new insulation and flooring. And, as Conley puts it, they are "making sure this ninety-year-old tin can continues to operate as efficiently as it can."

What they don't intend to do, though, is add to the dining car space—something that Conley says would take away from the classic diner. "What's wrong with that is then you have a dining room that has nothing to do with the appeal of the original location," Conley said. Though, he admits the diner would likely do even better if they did.

"We have [the kitchen addition built in the 1980s], and we're using storage in a building across the street. Eventually, we may add to the current kitchen, but for now, we don't have plans to do that," Conley said. The fifteen-foot kitchen, Conley said, "functions very well."

How Is the Corned Beef Hash?
So good that it was sold out when we visited. Seriously. So, plans are in the works to go again (a little earlier in the day) to try it.

Is Lobster on the Menu?
No.

Owner Favorite
Fried chicken sandwich

How to Get There
From I-95, take exit 36 for I-195 East toward Saco/Old Orchard Beach. Continue on I-195 for about 1.1 miles. Take exit 2A for US-1 South toward Saco/Downtown. Then follow Main Street until you reach Franklin Street in Biddeford. Turn left onto Franklin. The Palace Diner will be on your right. Parking is available in a lot.

DELUXE DINER (1928)

29 Oxford Avenue, Rumford

From the outside, it's a slim brick building with windows that is located in the mill town of Rumford. It's petite against the larger buildings that have been built up around it. Yet, there it stands, as it has since arriving in Rumford, Maine, in the late 1920s.

Step inside and you'll see the fine details of a Worcester Lunch Car Company dining car—one of three still in operation in Maine. The company built 651 diners between 1906 and 1961 in Worcester, Massachusetts.

Once it came off the assembly line in 1928, it was taken by rail to Essex Avenue in Rumford. According to a 2006 article in the *Lewiston Sun-Journal*, "From there, it was pulled up the hill to its Oxford Avenue site by a team of horses for owner Arthur Gastonguay. There, a crew hand-dug the cellar, then placed the dining car atop it."

According to a history of the diner compiled by Myrtle McKenna in 1989 and preserved by the Rumford Historical Society, "During the spring of that year (circa 1929), as soon as the frost was out of the ground, Dubois & Son started to dig the cellar by hand (pick & shovel). It was hard digging as there was a lot of rock. They had to drill into the rock and there was still some frost in the ground. It took 3 weeks to do the digging. The rocks were used in the walls of the foundation."

That hand-dug cellar still sits below the dining car.

Likewise, the original door—a sliding one—still opens for customers to enter. That feature is also one that lets folks know when an out-of-towner arrives and everyone should behave, says owner Jodi Campbell. "There's a whole chorus down the bar that says, 'slide it!'"

The Deluxe Diner is a little pocket of history, albeit one that hasn't gotten the same attention as other Worcester diners in Maine. Over the years, this small diner has been called the Rumford Diner, the Delux Diner and the Deluxe Diner. "We're tucked away. It's a small little mill town with a population of under seven thousand," Campbell said. "Thankfully for Google we do get a lot of people from out of town who come in."

Gastonguay, who added an extension to the kitchen, according to McKenna's history, owned the diner until the 1940s, when he sold it to Neri Cormier. Cormier sold the diner to Eddie and Lottie LaChapelle in 1947. The LaChapelles operated it for eighteen years, until 1965, when the diner was sold it to Tim Ronan. Meanwhile, Lottie LaChappelle, then widowed,

The Deluxe Diner in Rumford has been in the same location since it arrived in the late 1920s.

continued working at the diner for the next several years and owners. Ronan sold it to Raymond and Irene Richard in June 1971, but they didn't hold on to the diner for long. A few months later, in the fall of 1971, they sold it to John DeSalle. DeSalle, who put a new roof on the diner, operated it until February 1985. It was then leased to Faylene Austin, who later purchased it. Records are unclear from this time, but it appears that the diner closed from October 1986 until May 1987 or 1988, or possibly for an eight-month period during those years, when Peter and Jeanie Duguay bought it and reopened it.

Campbell and her sister Julie Kiley bought the Deluxe Diner in 2014 from Connie Arsenault, who'd owned it for a decade after purchasing it from the Duguays. Campbell had worked there before purchasing it, just as Arsenault had before her. And though the Deluxe Diner has a regular cast of locals who frequent the diner, owners Campbell and Kiley love that it draws folks from all over.

Rumford, incorporated in 1800, is one of the few towns in Maine that still boasts an operating paper mill. It's home to ND Paper, a pulp and paper mill that's been in operation since 1900. According to the U.S. Census Bureau's American Community Survey, Rumford's population was estimated to be 5,730 in 2017.

"It's just a sense of community here and I really, really appreciate that," Campbell said. There's a sense of community in the diner, too, in a town where "everyone knows everyone," Campbell said.

"Most of [the regulars] are old-timers, and they come in and they tell about the ailments and how the wife pissed them off last night," Campbell said.

Some, she said, even have a deeper history with the diner. "We have an old picture from the '40s that a customer gave us," Campbell said. The customer's father owned the diner, and she and her sister refer to trips there as "going to Daddy's place."

Now, though, it's really Campbell and Riley's place. And it's one with a little

An old menu from the Deluxe Diner, circa 1970s.

attitude and a lot of laughter. "We joke all day long. We're sometimes crass, we're sometimes mouthy and the customers enjoy that," Campbell said.

On the menu at the Deluxe Diner is classic diner food served for breakfast and lunch. There's eggs, bacon, sausage and ham. There's French toast and Deluxe steak 'n' eggs. And there's a whole list of omelets served with American cheese and toast. Plus, there's breakfast sandwiches, corned beef and more. Both Riley and Campbell said their homemade hash browns are the best around—and diners agree. For lunch, there's also burgers, sandwiches, chicken fingers and more.

Campbell, who does the cooking at the grill behind the counter, makes everything to order however the diners like it. But it wasn't that long ago that she didn't even know how to cook. "I learned to cook from watching the prior cook. I learned from the owner....It was a real learning curve at first," Campbell said. Turns out, though, that she loved it. "It's just so much fun."

So, the woman who says she "never had the inclination to own a restaurant" bought one with her sister—and a quirky one at that. The sliding door isn't the only classic touch in the Deluxe Diner. "I think people were much smaller [ninety years ago]," Campbell laughed. The close-together stools, which have patrons literally rubbing shoulders at times, are part of the charm.

Other details—like the original subway tile and the marble counters—are things the sisters keep with pride. "The subway tile is cracked, but it's all

Left: Corned beef hash at the Deluxe Diner, shown with the signature hash browns, eggs over easy and homemade wheat toast.

Below: Sisters Jodi Campbell and Julie Kiley own the Deluxe Diner in Rumford.

original, so we won't mess with it," Campbell said. "We have a German silver hood that we polish up every week."

And though so much hasn't changed about the Deluxe Diner, some things have. The original silver exterior isn't visible anymore, and though former owner Arsenault told the *Sun-Journal* she'd like to restore it, that didn't happen.

These days, Campbell and Kiley aim to keep up with the upkeep of the ninety-year-old diner, which is no small feat. "It's an awful lot, and it takes its toll," Campbell said. But it's worth it too. The highlight of owning the Deluxe Diner comes in the atmosphere and the act of feeding people, Campbell said.

"We come from an Italian family, and food was love," Campbell said. "That's how we express our [love] for each other was through food."

She also appreciates how the diner has brought her sister out of her shell. Kiley is the waitress and keeps customers chatting throughout the day. "There's just the counter here, there's no tables. The familiarity you get very quickly. Just chatting people up," Campbell said. "The next time they come in, you call them by name."

How Is the Corned Beef Hash?
Good. Mine came perfectly crispy all over. Campbell says asking for it well done will get it like that.

Is Lobster on the Menu?
No.

Owner Favorite
"A steak and cheese omelet with home fries. Also, a bacon cheeseburger. We buy a top of the round and shave it for steaks and grind it for burgers. Really good!"

—Jodi Campbell

How to Get There
The Deluxe Diner is off the beaten path, so your best bet is to use GPS. However, if you'd rather, here's how to get there: From I-95, take exit 109B for US-202 West/ME-11 West/ME-17 West/ME-100 West toward Winthrop. Follow ME-100 South/ME-11 South/ME-17 West/US-202 West for 8.9 miles. Turn right onto Western Avenue. Continue on that road (it becomes Lake Street) until you

reach ME-133 North. Make a slight left onto ME-133 North and follow that road for 5.9 miles. Make a left onto ME-219 West and follow it for 5.7 miles. Turn right onto ME-108 West and follow ME-108 West for about 26.0 miles. (There will be a few times you have to turn to stay on 108. Do it.) Turn right onto Franklin Street (it becomes Rumford Avenue) and then left onto Hancock Street and then right onto Oxford Street.

MOODY'S DINER (1934)

1885 Atlantic Highway, Waldoboro
moodysdiner.com

It was built slowly. What would become Moody's Diner started as a small lunch wagon in the early 1930s. It was located on what's now Route 1A next to a small restaurant the Moody family had opened to serve breakfast and dinner to travelers staying at their cabins.

But really, the business dates a little further back, to 1927, when Percy and Bertha Moody opened three small one-room cabins. There wasn't running water, and guests used dry toilets out back. More cabins were eventually added. Then showers and toilets and eventually woodstoves for heat.

When the state rerouted Route 1, the Moodys purchased land on the new road so they could connect their business with it via a road they built. "We moved the little lunch wagon down to the new Route 1, put a screened porch on the front, and were ready for business when the new road opened," Bertha Moody wrote in 1976, the year before she died. Her history of Moody's Diner is printed in *What's Cooking at Moody's Diner* by her daughter Nancy Moody Genthner. The book includes recipes, photos, stories and more.

Over the years, the family, which grew to include nine children, added to Moody's little by little until the restaurant was a robust space. First it was an addition on the back with restrooms, and then a woodshed.

"In 1949, we moved the back wall of the kitchen out five feet," wrote Alvah Moody in *What's Cooking at Moody's Diner*. "I took the crew over on a Saturday night and we cut the wall right out, put it on some pipes and rolled it right out. We studded up the roof, left the fans on the wall and had an electrician extend the wiring, and started cooking in the new space the next morning."

The Moody's Diner sign at night has beckoned to many hungry passersby over the years.

The most recent renovation was in 1994 and 1995, when Genthner told the *Bangor Daily News* that the family had extended the restaurant "about 16 feet to the west and about 10 feet out all along the back." The roof was also raised, new duct work was put in for a better heating and cooling system and the building was rewired. Today, the restaurant can serve about one hundred people—a significant increase from its lunch cart roots.

But the heart of the diner remains. It's been family-run since the business began. Today, a family corporation oversees it and about twenty family members work in the diner—from general manager Dan Beck to the dishwashing staff. "It's still family owned and operated....We have up to the fifth generation working here," Beck said. Beck owns it with his uncle Alvah Moody, aunt Genthner and cousin Steve.

All told, the diner is a major employer for the Waldoboro area. "We employee, depending on the season, anywhere from 60 to 85 people," Beck said. About half of those work full time.

But it's more than that. It's an icon on the midcoast that has welcomed hungry folks since the 1930s. And it's a place that draws a variety of regulars. Among the many folks who pass through Moody's doors each year are beloved regulars like the late Woody Verge, who died in 2018 at age 101.

The former school bus driver had been eating at Moody's every morning for much of his life and is the first person who comes to Beck's mind when thinking about regulars. "Woody was a regular in here every single day," Beck said. "Most people will have some critics. Woody didn't have any."

Moody's Diner was even mentioned in Woody's obituary on ObitTree. com. "Every morning, Woody could be found sitting in 'his booth' at Moody's Diner. He was one of Moody's first customers, eating at their original location on Old Route 1 in Waldoboro. He had the menu memorized and knew all the specials," the obituary states. "The waitresses were 'his girls' and the entire staff was like extended family to him. He looked forward to spending time with them every day and was so happy to spend his birthdays at Moody's with his family and friends."

Woody wasn't alone as a devoted patron of Moody's. "We have a contingent of these older, faithful regulars. We are growing a generation of younger regulars," Beck said. "They are part of the fabric of the Moody's family."

Perhaps it's no surprise that this diner with such strong family ties and devotion would draw folks year after year. It is familiar. "We value the family tradition. We have great respect for our grandparents and what they did," Beck said. "We want to do what we can to carry on that legacy."

With a lot of real wood and wood-tone paneling, making the diner seem like a log cabin, and a country feel, right down to the plaid curtains, the diner has a feeling of home. Customers belly up to the old Formica countertop that has greeted folks for decades and sit in green, spinning stools with backs. Nearby, familiar booths hold more folks.

Although the diner has undergone many renovations over the years, it has also aimed to keep things the same for regulars who love it just as it is. "We have the same straight back, uncomfortable booths that we've had for decades. We have the same yellow laminate countertop that we've had for decades," Beck said.

Over the years, the diner has undergone some necessary changes behind the scenes, including using a computer for orders, accepting credit cards and changing the operating hours. While Moody's was once—not unlike L.L. Bean—open twenty-four hours each day, that stopped in 2000. Over the years, the closing time was moved up little by little. These days, Moody's is open until 9:00 p.m.

The Moody's menu is expansive and includes a wide selection of breakfast foods and lunch and dinner options. "The Reuben is probably one of my favorite sandwiches. We get our sauerkraut from Morse's Sauerkraut, which is right here in Waldoboro," Beck said. The sandwich can be ordered with

The corned beef Rueben sandwich at Moody's Diner is made with house-made corned beef.

corned beef, pastrami or turkey. As for the customers, he says that the hot turkey sandwich, made with Moody's own roast turkey—made nightly—and homemade gravy, is among the most popular.

"What we've become known for is our pies. Our bakers come in between two and three in the morning and they work until the work is done," Beck said. And that baking staff bakes quite a bit—including fifty to sixty pies daily, as well as whoopie pies, cakes, muffins and donuts.

As for the breakfast menu, Beck loves the item called simply "the Breakfast," a title that his son, a U.S. Marine, suggested. It includes sausage gravy and a biscuit, two eggs, a Cheddarwurst sausage and home fries. Like the corned beef hash and poached eggs, it's only available until 11:00 a.m. each day. Most breakfast items, though, are served all day long.

As for accomplishments, Moody's has many, including being featured on television shows, being named the 2015 Restauranteur of the Year by the Maine Restaurant Association and being chosen in readers' polls by local publication the *Village Soup* for having the best pie. It has also been picked as the readers' and editors' pick for the best diner in Maine.

But Beck says it's the staying power of the diner and the people behind it that are the highlights of the restaurant's history. "I think we survive each summer—I say that jokingly but seriously," Beck said. In the winter, most days, the diner serves between 500 and 800 people. In the summer, that balloons to between 1,100 and 1,400 each day.

Moody's Diner is located on Route 1 in Waldoboro.

Beck credits the family's strong faith with keeping everything going. "It takes a lot of effort, a lot of time and commitment, a lot of energy to keep this place going," Beck said. "You run a business like this, and there is always the unexpected that's going to happen."

The supportive regulars—both locals and summer folks—don't hurt either. "Every summer, we're seeing a new trend of regulars where Moody's has become not just a place to stop by. It's become a destination point," Beck said.

Those regulars are bringing a little bit of Moody's around the globe. Photos of folks wearing Moody's Diner shirts at locations around the world line the walls of the diner. It's all part of carrying on what Percy and Bertha Moody started so many years ago. "We want to do what we can to carry on that legacy," Beck said. And so, they do.

How Is the Corned Beef Hash?
I don't know. Moody's only serves corned beef hash until 11:00 a.m. However, I have had their Reuben with corned beef, and it was delightful. If that's any indication, I'll bet the corned beef hash is pretty good too.

Is Lobster on the Menu?
Yes, there's a lobster roll, lobster chef salad and lobster stew. Also, Monday's mac and cheese special can be lobster mac and cheese by request and with an extra fee.

Owner Favorite
Dan Beck has a few, but particularly special to him is the Breakfast— so named by his son. "My son, who is a marine, said, 'Dad, you need to put this on the menu. Just call it "the Breakfast,"'" Beck said. It includes sausage gravy and a biscuit, two eggs, a Cheddarwurst sausage and home fries.

How to Get There
From I-295, take exit 28 and merge onto US-1 North toward Coastal Route/Brunswick Bath. Stay on US-1 North for about thirty-seven miles. Moody's will be on your right.

2
Mid-Century Diners

Mills continued to employ many people in Maine through the mid-twentieth century, even as some industries began to decamp for other less expensive locations. Many of the textile mills in the Biddeford and Saco areas, for instance, closed as new ones opened much closer to the cotton in the South. But in some communities, the need for restaurants catering to mill workers continued.

Meanwhile, the State of Maine was doubling down on its allure as a vacation spot. It was in the mid-1960s that the moniker "Vacationland" was adopted by the state to draw more folks to its beloved craggy shoreline. And on the road there, more diners popped up to serve the traveling masses.

A1 DINER (1946)
3 Bridge Street, Gardiner

The metal dining car stands on strong girders, where it's been for more than seventy-two years. Inside, a clock rimmed in blue neon permanently says 1:35, and a handwritten note in the center calls this "Diner Time."

Blue and black tiles, spinning stools at the counter and a wall covered in dark wood and stainless—this diner looks the part. Listen as folks come and go, and you'll hear that this is, indeed, the real deal.

The A1 Diner opened as Heald's Diner in 1946.

The Worcester Lunch Car Company diner was No. 790 when it was built in Worcester, Massachusetts, in 1946. It was made-to-order based on the specifications carefully selected by its first owner, Eddie Heald.

Heald, who had opened Bridge Street Lunch in 1937, had ordered the dining car to modernize his eatery. When it arrived in Gardiner, the front of the Bridge Street Lunch building was removed, and the diner was carefully fitted. To do so took special efforts—steel girders custom built by Ralph Dick of T.W. Dick steel company in Gardiner. It was a unique solution to put the diner at street level, and one that remains to this day.

Owner Aaron Harris, who purchased the diner in 2018, says the unusual placement is something that catches the eyes of passersby—and brings some people in. "The manner in which the diner sits is part of what makes the diner cool," Harris said. "[It's] probably the only Worcester dining car that's sitting on steel beams."

The exterior of the diner remains the ivory porcelain emblazoned with Heald's in red Old English lettering. And though it's obscured by the bridge railing, it also says "Counter Service," something still offered in the classic diner.

Marguerite Gagne, Heald's daughter, told the author of *A1 Diner*, a history and cookbook, that her father had ordered the top-of-the-line diner. "That was the best one you could buy," Gagne said.

The A1 Diner in Gardiner sits on steel girders that make it level with the bridge.

Both Bridge Street Lunch and Heald's, which replaced it, catered to the folks working at nearby mills and factories in Gardiner and quickly served up hot meals throughout the day.

Heald didn't run the diner for long. In fact, just six years later, in 1952, he sold it to Maurice Wakefield, who changed the name, naturally, to Wakefield's. Wakefield's continued the tradition of serving food hot and fast but also increased the emphasis on fresh foods.

When Wakefield was ready to retire, word got around, and Albert Giberson heard about it. On a whim, he and his wife, Elizabeth, bought it in 1979. "He kind of bought it as a retirement business, and I think he soon realized it was not a retirement business," Michael Giberson, his son, said. "I was a little shocked when he bought it. And like the previous owner, Giberson changed the name of the diner to the Giberson Diner.

In 1987, Mike Giberson and his partner, Neil Anderson, took over the diner. In 1988, they renamed it the A1 Diner. The name came from a red-and-yellow neon sign Anderson bought for Michael Giberson in a Cape Cod antique shop. That sign still hangs behind the counter today.

Giberson said that changing the name was an act of symbolism. "The diner up until that point was old school. The food was just generic—there

Inside the A1 Diner, built-in stools line the counter that runs the length of the dining car.

were a lot of frozen products and cost-cutting measures to make the place more profitable. We wanted to change the name to let people know that there was a change in ownership, and things were going to be different," Giberson said.

It worked. These days an array of regulars order big, fresh burgers with crispy fries; stuffed sandwiches with chips and a pickle; and a special A1 blend of coffee from Maine roaster Wicked Joe. As they arrive, the waitstaff greets them with familiarity and asks if they want their regular orders. The staff even knows backup orders.

With a focus on fresh, local and creative diner fare, the A1 Diner draws crowds of local regulars, seasonal regulars and passersby. Sure, it has the corned beef hash and pancakes, but it also has an array of sandwiches like grilled turkey, brie and apple butter and grilled gruyere and caramelized onions, as well as creative burgers, wraps and more on the regular menu, plus a rotating array of specials.

To get there, though, took a slow shift from the old menu his father had created to a new one that emphasized fresh, local and sometimes creative offerings. "We walked a fine line when we changed [the menu] because you don't want to alienate the existing customers you have but you want to attract a younger clientele. We needed younger people," Giberson said.

The menu changes were gradual—first simply improving on the dishes the diner already served and later adding their own spin on things. "We started getting good reviews. We got written up in the Sunday paper from Portland, and then we ended up in a little blurb in the *New York Times*, and then it kind of went on from there," Giberson said.

Giberson credits the location—a crossroads of sorts where two Maine highways meet—as partly responsible for the diner's success. "People would drive right by our diner," Giberson said, so they worked to draw in the tourism traffic. "Our clientele is really varied," Giberson said. "The good thing about a diner is that everyone feels comfortable walking in. I think it's a great place for single people because you can sit at the counter and meet people....We have so many regular customers and so many repeat customers; it's amazing."

But it wasn't just the comfort of a diner that drew folks back for more— it was the food. Before farm-to-table was a popular restaurant concept, Giberson began buying local produce and goods for the diner.

"It was in the early 2000s. We started being approached by local farmers and people who grew apples and foraged mushrooms. Whenever we were approached by anybody, we were like 'Yep, we'll take it and please bring more,'" Giberson said. "No one thought of it as farm-to-table then. We just thought of it as nice, fresh produce."

When farmers markets began springing up around the area and around Maine, they would also shop there for ingredients. "We really didn't realize we were part of a new movement, but we certainly were," Giberson said.

Now, the same farmer has provided many in-season vegetables for the past twenty-five years. A second farm has filled in the supply gaps for them. "Not everything we serve is fresh and local because we're in a state where the growing season is short. We do what we can," Giberson said.

And the menu gets changed from time to time. "We get tired of making the same things, and we stop, and then years later, we'll run across the recipe again and then sell it again," Giberson said.

Corned beef hash at the A1 Diner.

But sometimes the changes to the menu are more cosmetic. That was the case with a chicken sandwich. It just wasn't selling well, so they decided to keep it but change the name to the "Undertaker's Wife" because the local undertaker's wife loved it. "Now it sells like crazy," Giberson laughed. "It seems everything we make sells well, and if it doesn't sell well, we change the name."

Other times, they'll add new items to the specials board that are inspired by their travels. Such was the case with avocado fries, which are breaded and fried slices of avocado. "We kind of stole it from a restaurant in Toronto. It's really popular," Giberson said.

The really popular items on the specials board sometimes end up becoming regular menu items. "When we drop something off the printed menu and are looking for something to replace it with, that's when we think of what's been popular on the specials board," Giberson said.

If you go, leave room for dessert. They are made by Giberson's sister and change frequently. In the past, they've included gingerbread with lemon sauce, Mexican chocolate cheesecake, pecan pie and warm brownie cups à la mode.

For Giberson, though, he's completed his last shift. He's selling the business to "someone who loves and respects the diner as much as we do. We didn't have to put it on the market. This guy just wanted to buy it." And that offers peace of mind to the man who's been a devoted diner owner for thirty years.

"When you've owned it for thirty years, you want to pass it on to someone who respects what you've done," Giberson said.

That's precisely what they found in Harris, a former employee, who returned to purchase the diner. When Harris bought the diner in late 2018, his aim was to carry on the legacy Giberson and Harris had begun. "The diner is so special that I don't want it to change. It's the place that gave my life purpose when I came to Maine eight years ago," Harris said.

Harris moved to Maine from Illinois in 2001, following his family who'd already moved to the area. "I thought I was going to go to culinary school," Harris said. In the meantime, though, he wasn't really sure what he was doing. "Mom said, 'There's this great little restaurant down the hill. If you want to go to culinary school, you should check it out.'"

That little restaurant was the A1 Diner, and Harris was enamored. "It was so unique and so charming," Harris said.

Soon, he was working there, learning both the front and the back of house. Harris credits Giberson and Anderson with teaching him "everything I know" and making him "feel like part of a family."

It was at the diner where Harris met the woman who would become his wife. After they were married, Harris felt like he "needed to get real with life." So, he went to college and got a degree in marketing. From there, he worked in corporate marketing at a law firm for eight years. Occasionally, he'd work a shift at the diner too. "When Michael's mother passed away, I came in and cooked a shift for him so he could go to the funeral," Harris said.

About five or six years into his career as a marketing professional, something just didn't feel right. That's when Harris first approached Giberson, asking if he'd "ever think of selling." The answer was yes—but not yet. A few years later though, in 2018, the time was right, and the two came to an agreement.

"It was very informal. We sat in his backyard and had this amazing drink he whipped up, came to price and terms," Harris recalled. Then they got their lawyers involved to finalize things and draw up contracts. "I love this place, and it did something for me that no other job had done."

For Giberson, it's time for another act of his life. "I'm not the retiring type. I turned sixty-seven yesterday, but I don't want to retire," Giberson said in October 2018. He's hoping to travel to Italy and perhaps get another job. His husband will continue working, which "kind of gives me freedom to do what I want.

After three decades, it's time for that. "We work like slaves, and we're tied to our business twenty-four seven, so it will be a real change for me and nice to have a different kind of life," Giberson said.

Harris plans to continue to evolve with the times—perhaps even experimenting with Maine beers and wines, which he thinks might just be the next big thing. One thing that won't change is the commitment to local, fresh food. "It's just great to keep money in the community, and it makes such a difference," Harris said.

But it's not all economic. Harris said there's also what he calls a "selfish reason." The locally grown produce just tastes better. Plus, he loves seeing the farmers when they come in because they are "do it yourself, driven, independent people."

In the winter, when there's much less locally grown produce available, the diner will continue doing what it can, like using local eggs and purchasing baked goods from a small local baker. It will also be a family affair. "My whole family is involved in this. My wife, Sarah, is helping out with all the bookkeeping, all the payroll. A lot of the soul of the place is my wife," Harris said. He'll be running the kitchen. And their kids—Olivia, Spencer and Eleanor—are also excited. "They love the place as much as I do," Harris said.

Along with the change of ownership will come other changes for the diner. The bridge it sits next to will be torn down and replaced in 2020, but the building will stay right where it is. In fact, the Maine Department of Transportation is making sure it does. "They are making all these safety precautions to protect the diner," Giberson said.

What won't change is the food. Harris believes in the fresh, local menu that has been feeding diners well for decades. "A1 Diner is the A1 Diner," Harris said. "I feel like sort of a steward in a way because I hope it's here when I am not. I do own it, but I am conscious of the fact that the community owns it as much as I do."

How Is the Corned Beef Hash?
Fresh corned beef with lots and lots of potatoes. It's a different take on the classic. But the A1 Diner has so many great, fresh dishes on the menu, you can't go wrong with any of the creative options.

Is Lobster on the Menu?
Not the regular menu, but it sometimes appears in specials.

Owner Favorite
Former owner Michael Giberson loved the fish tacos.

How to Get There
Take exit 51 off I-95. Turn left onto ME-9/ME-126 toward Gardiner. Continue on that road for 3.16 miles. Turn left onto Bridge Street (US-201 North). The diner will be on your right.

BRUNSWICK DINER (1946)

101.5 Pleasant Street, Brunswick

On Route 1 in Brunswick is a red, barrel-roofed diner that has welcomed folks into its intimate, warm space since the 1940s. The Brunswick Diner, now owned by Jane Davis, is a well-preserved glimpse into mid-century diners.

Built in the late 1930s, in Norway, Maine, this building was once the Norway Diner. Although it was once believed to be a Worcester Lunch Car Company dining car, it's not. Charles S. Longley, the sometimes curator for the Norway Historical Society, said it was actually hand-built on site.

"A short notice in the *Norway Advertiser-Democrat* for 22 December 1939 states that Pierce Chappelle [C. Pierce Chappelle] of Lewiston was building a diner on a vacant cellar foundation between J.J. Newberry and Z.L. Merchant," Longley said. "The building was to be one story high with a frontage of forty feet facing Main Street. Chappelle was a well-known and popular horse trainer and driver in the pacing and trotting racing circuit."

Another notice a week later "notes that Chappelle's 'modern diner' on Main Street was fast taking form and noted that John E. Jacobsen of Norway was 'boss carpenter,'" Longley said.

The diner, with a design similar to the popular Worcester dining cars, celebrated its opening on February 14, 1940. It's unclear how long Chappelle owned the diner, but according to an obituary for Doris Bragg Buchanan in the *Sun-Journal* in 2008, Buchanan and her husband, Robert, owned and operated the Norway Diner after they were married in 1940. The couple also farmed and grew food to supply the diner, according to the obituary. After selling the business, the Buchanans moved to Fort Myers, Florida, before returning to settle in Auburn.

Meanwhile, the diner moved as well. Less than a decade after its construction, in 1948, the Norway Diner was sold and moved to Brunswick. The so-called modern diner found a new home along a busy stretch of road.

The Brunswick Diner, formerly the Norway Diner and Norwego Diner, has stood at 101.5 Pleasant Street since the late 1940s.

"The [Norway Historical] Society has an unsourced newspaper clipping showing the diner on wheels about to be moved, and a short notice under the photo notes that the twelve-by-forty-foot diner 'took to wheels' on Thursday for Brunswick, where owner Robert Buchanan was to open it for business," Longley said. "An article in the *Norway Advertiser-Democrat* [on January 9, 1948] reported that the diner had been removed from its foundation and blocked up on the sidewalk on Wednesday (7 January) and mounted on a wheeled carriage and started on its journey to Brunswick on Thursday (8 January)."

The diner was moved to 101.5 Pleasant Street, also known as Route 1, where it has remained ever since. According to the Brunswick directory from 1949, it was named the Norwago Diner, a moniker it retained until 1972, when owner Ed Buckley changed it to the Miss Brunswick Diner. In 1975, for the first time, the diner at 101.5 Pleasant Street was referred to as the Miss Brunswick Diner in the Brunswick directory. Eventually, it dropped the "Miss" from its name.

But it wasn't the first time there had been a diner called the Miss Brunswick in this historic town. Alcide Thibeault had also owned a Miss Brunswick Diner on Pleasant Street. His was located at number 16 and operated until

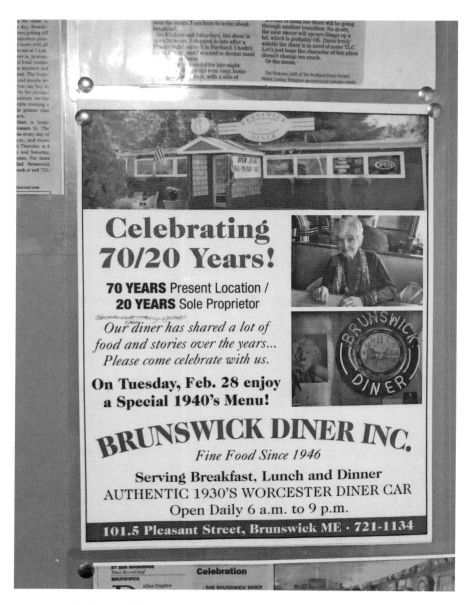

The Brunswick Diner celebrated its owner's twentieth year of ownership and its seventieth year at 101.5 Pleasant Street in 2018.

at least 1951. "[Thibeault] set up the Miss Brunswick Diner in the mid-1930s and tore it down in 1953 to make way for a store," wrote Richard F. Snow in *A History of Four Brunswick Streets*. That Miss Brunswick Diner, sometimes confused with the modern Brunswick Diner, was a different restaurant in a different location.

These days, entering the snug, intimate space at 101.5 Pleasant Street, folks slide into booths and saddle up to counter stools. The red-and-blue checkerboard tile floor lines the space, keeping it clean and unique. But that seems to be the theme of this diner, where an orange-and-yellow sunburst is painted on the otherwise white ceiling. Squat counter stools with red vinyl covering await customers. Booths with worn wood-like Formica countertops serve even more. The dining room is long and narrow but well taken care of. Mirrors make it feel bigger and broader. A neon illuminated Brunswick Diner clock hangs at the center of the car—a centerpiece to the bustling activity inside. Mugs hang from the wall behind the counter. Vintage Coke bottles decorate a shelf at one end of the car.

Regulars are greeted with familiarity and conversation. On a Saturday evening in the summertime, people come and go with just enough frequency that there isn't a line, but there aren't free seats for long. A tiny window behind the counter—squat and maybe two feet long—gives a view into the cooking area. The sounds of faucets, dishes clanging and glass cups provide a soundtrack.

For more than seventy years, the Brunswick Diner has been feeding folks along this stretch of Route 1—the gateway to the midcoast. Davis bought the Brunswick Diner more than twenty years ago from Andre and Cathleen Prest, who had renovated it but closed it after operating it for two years. "It's been in the present location for over seventy years," Davis said. Larry B. and Fay Ann Smith owned it before the Prests. The Smiths purchased the diner in 1986 and ran it for ten years.

The diner used to attract truckers, who lined Route 1 with their eighteen-wheelers when they stopped in for a hot meal, Davis said. "It used to be one of the famous truck stops on Route 1," Davis said.

These days, it has a cast of regulars who are part of the daily flow. "Some regulars come in two times a day. It's kind of like home for them. They eat their meals there, and then meet their friends there," Davis said. "There's a six o'clock crowd that comes in…they sit in the same booth and one guy; we had a sign up for a while [with a picture], 'if you see this man, get up. It's his booth.'"

The vibe is welcoming, and folks have been coming here for years. "All these men, they come every morning, and they catch up with each other," Davis said. Those men who used to drop in on their way to work are now retired, but they are still coming in.

There's even a coffee club at the diner—a caffeinated version of neighborhood bar mug clubs, where folks have "their" mug that they use each time they come in. "So, they all have their mugs hanging. The girls will get their mugs out and have them ready," Davis said.

These days, the regulars are so familiar that they're like family. When one regular doesn't show up for a while, the waitresses check in. "If somebody doesn't show up in the morning, they'll call them just to make sure they're OK," Davis said. "We've had people who come every day. There's one gal who didn't show up for a few days. She was sick." When the staff learned that, they brought her food.

That level of caring and concern is what sets the Brunswick Diner apart, Davis says. And it's what has kept her in the business—not food service but the human service. "I really have no business in the restaurant business, but the people business I seem to like," Davis laughed.

When Davis purchased the diner, she was a single mother with a daughter in elementary school. The business offered her a way to work and care for her daughter. "She could get picked up by the bus right out front. She went to a little private Christian school in Woolwich," Davis recalled. "She just loved it. I was there [at the diner] full time. She never had to go to daycare. It was just perfect."

As her daughter grew, she went on to work at the diner when she was a teenager—something that came naturally to the kid who grew up there. "She learned a lot at a very young age," Davis said.

In recent years, Davis has re-staffed the Brunswick Diner. Two or three folks have been there for twenty years, and the rest have been there for eight to ten years. The Brunswick Diner has about twelve employees in the winter and eighteen in the summer. Business picks up a lot in those warm months, when coastal Maine–bound travelers pass by.

"We try to create a family atmosphere. I'm lucky because a lot of the staff, they are friends with each other and they are friends with the customers," Davis said.

But it's a challenging time for small businesses, as the cost of doing business rises and the expectations of untrained, entry-level workers grow. "It's getting more and more expensive to run a small business, and it's almost impossible to staff it," Davis said. "We were doing twenty-four hours, and it was great. It was really busy at night."

Corned beef hash at the Brunswick Diner.

However, without enough staff and being unable to pay overtime, the diner cut back on hours and had to reconsider pricing—but all within reason. After all, the Brunswick Diner is still, ultimately, a diner. "I can't sell a fifteen-dollar burger at the Brunswick Diner," Davis said. Prices remain wallet friendly.

These days, the Brunswick Diner is back to basics, with a working jukebox and a timeless menu. The jukebox, in particular, was recently restored thanks to a customer with some experience. "It probably took him six months of tinkering. He rewired everything," Davis said. "It became his little baby." Now customers can slide in a quarter, select a song and play it—just like the old days.

Davis has heard many rumors of famous folks who've dropped in for a bite at the Brunswick Diner over the years. Names like Frank Sinatra and Glenn Close ring bells for many people. But it's the locals who ingrain themselves in the day-to-day of the diner. "It's really quite a local icon," Davis said.

The food at the Brunswick Diner is what Davis calls "real basic diner food." Meals like liver and onions and meatloaf are favorites among the customers. "It took two years for folks to start buying our mimosas," Davis laughed. "People just want basic [food]. That's what our customers are after."

Still, the menu now includes eggs benedict. And the specials sometimes include lobster. But the menu is filled with good, basic food. It features an all-day breakfast, lunch and dinner menu, including dishes like mega three-egg omelets; homemade favorites, like the James Dean (sausage gravy with a kick over a biscuit, served with two eggs any style); and dinners like Miss B's homemade meatloaf.

As for Davis, she likes the basics. "For me, well, I love our omelets and the assorted omelets, and I love our hash and eggs. We make a really good hash and eggs," Davis said.

What is it that makes the Brunswick Diner special? "That connection with the customers and the friendliness," Davis said. "I've told the girls that we're the hostess. We're hosting people here. Treat people like they are coming to your house."

So, they say hello to everyone who comes in and dish out hugs to the ones they know. And they deliver good, wholesome food with a friendly attitude. "They know they are going to get a good value.…[When] people go to a diner, they know what they're getting," Davis said.

If you go, bring cash. They don't accept cards or checks. But don't panic if you forget—there is an ATM in the dining car.

How Is the Corned Beef Hash?
If you are a fan of corned beef, this one is worth trying. It's the typical canned fare, but it is cooked well. A nicely crisped outside and soft center make a lovely dish that is perfect with runny eggs over easy.

Is Lobster on the Menu?
A lobster roll is sometimes available.

Owner Favorite
Davis loves the omelets and the hash and eggs, but she also really loves the liver and onions.

How to Get There
From I-295 South, take exit 31A and merge onto Lewiston Road/ME-196 East toward Topsham/Brunswick. Turn right onto US-201 South (Main Street) for 1.34 miles. Merge onto US-1 toward I-295/Portland. The Brunswick Diner will be on the left.

MISS PORTLAND DINER (1949)

140 Marginal Way, Portland
missportlanddiner.com

The red neon "diner" sign can be seen from the highway—a call to travelers heading north that there's a familiar place off the next exit.

Just off the highway in the Bayside neighborhood of Portland sits the Miss Portland Diner, a 1949 Worcester Lunch Car Company diner that has been attached to a modern addition, expanding the dining area and kitchen. The restored diner, with its blue exterior and gold lettering ("Miss Portland" sandwiched between two "Booth Service" mentions), sits on a tree-shaded stretch of Marginal Way in Portland.

Step through the doors, which are in the new part of the diner, and you might miss the dining car. But wise folks know to ask to sit there and to head right through a narrow passageway and up some stairs.

The barrel-roofed car has both booths and counter seats, with a marble counter, metal-edged Formica tabletops, a tiled floor and an old-fashion specials board with letters that slide into place. It's a clean, well-cared-for space with rich mahogany wood and blue leather. The waitresses, whether you sit at the counter or in a booth, are friendly and fun. And it's busy. The Miss Portland Diner draws a hungry crowd all year.

The Worcester Lunch Car Company built 651 diners in its factory in Worchester, Massachusetts, between 1906 and 1961 and numbered them beginning with 200. The Miss Portland Diner was No. 818. When it arrived in 1949, it was advertised as "Maine's Largest and Most Stream-Lined Diner."

You enter the Miss Portland Diner through the new part of the building. Step to the right and up the stairs, and you'll find the pristinely preserved Worcester Lunch Car No. 818.

The Miss Portland Diner, a classic Worcester Lunch Car Company dining car, is located on Marginal Way.

The Miss Portland Diner had its grand opening on Monday, March 7, 1949. It was owned by Jimmie Crowder Jr. and was located at 175 Forest Avenue, "just below the post office," according to an ad published in the *Portland Press Herald* on its opening day. The diner boasted twenty-four-hour service and ample parking. Opening day specials included roast Vermont Tom turkey served with potato and vegetables for seventy-five cents and old-fashioned New England beef stew with crackers and pickles for forty-five cents. There was also the Miss Portland special Bar B-Q beef with vegetables and potatoes for sixty-five cents, among several others.

Crowder, who died on August 5, 2006, at age eighty-one, had served in the merchant marines aboard the *Diamond Island*, according to his obituary. The ship exploded in Portland Harbor in 1946, and he was severely injured but survived and recovered over the next several years.

In 1964, the Miss Portland Diner moved to 49 Marginal Way. A new federal building was planned for Forest Avenue, and the diner had to be moved to make way. New owners Harold Foley and Albert Karas reopened the diner in its new location. It was bustling. In 2004, the *Portland Press Herald* ran a quote from an old interview in which Karas said, "There were times when we used to do 1,000 customers a day." Karas died in 1999.

Randall Chasse became the owner of the Miss Portland Diner in 1981. In 1993, the diner went smokeless—a significant change for a place that once housed the vending machine that sold the most cigarettes of any in the city.

Chasse attempted to sell the diner through an essay contest in 1994, according to the *Portland Press Herald*. Folks had to submit a 250-word essay about why they'd want to own and operate the diner and submit it with a $100 entry fee.

Chasse was "looking for someone who shares his commitment to the essential elements of diner fare: quality food, low prices and good nutrition," according to an article published in the *Bangor Daily News* in 1993. But Chasse failed to receive the five thousand entries he hoped for, and it wasn't sold.

In 2001, Chasse, then sixty, tried to sell again—this time via eBay auction. He was ready for retirement. The auction, however, included the business and some of the equipment. It didn't include the ten-thousand-square-foot property it sat on. "We just want to see what's out there," Chasse told the *Portland Press Herald*. "After all these years, it's time to do something else."

The ten-day auction received no bids. By 2004, Chasse decided to close the diner. The land was sold to a builder. "He sold the land out from under the diner," current owner Tom Manning said. However, the builder who purchased the land said the diner could remain until he was ready to build.

On March 14, 2004, one week after its fifty-fifth anniversary of opening in Portland, the Miss Portland Diner closed. Customers took the opportunity to celebrate the establishment. The *Boston Globe* wrote, "All week they streamed in, hungry and mournful, for one last taste of glory: their last meat loaf sandwich (hot or cold), their last corned beef hash (fat trimmed from the brisket), their last hand-cut fries (off the grill, not the frialator). They came to eat and to kibbitz but above all to say their respectful farewells to Mary and Randall and what customer Beth Holmes called 'a part of our culture.'"

Chasse donated the diner car to the City of Portland. Although he said he received some interest from folks out of state, he didn't want the Miss Portland to be anywhere other than Portland. In exchange, he received a tax write-off for the donation. "I want it to stay in Portland so that people can keep coming for another 55 years," Chasse told the *Boston Globe*.

City officials, who had to mull over the idea of accepting the donation, also saw the value in keeping the Miss Portland in Portland. "There is strong interest in the community in keeping the diner in Portland and possibly in Bayside," city councilor James Cloutier, head of the council's community development committee, told the *Portland Press Herald*.

The city received letters of interest from twelve people in Portland and around Maine with proposals for the diner. "The new owner or operator was expected to maintain the 818th creation of the Worcester Lunch Car Co. as an architectural and historical landmark. The diner and its interior would be designated as an individual landmark under the city's historic preservation ordinance. Any alterations or additions would be subject to city approval," the *Portland Press Herald* wrote in July 2004.

The city entered into negotiations with a potential owner, but that deal eventually fell through. That's when Manning decided to express interest. "It hit me one day in 2005 walking up Eighth Avenue on my way to work at *Newsweek*. During my bus ride from New Jersey, I'd been reading the online edition of the *Portland Press Herald*, the paper from my hometown in Portland, Maine. For months I'd been following the story of a local landmark diner, closed for several years, that was being sold by the city to someone with a plan to bring it back to life. That morning, I read that the pending deal had fallen through. And somewhere during my walk from 42nd Street to 57th Street, I decided to buy it," Manning wrote in an essay published in *Newsweek* in 2008.

Ten years later, he recognized how much he didn't know before owning the diner. "I didn't think I would have to be there all the time, but I am a businessperson. You are almost married to it. You have to be there all the

The interior of the Miss Portland Diner's lunch car is well maintained and draws a crowd.

time," Manning said. "I have managers, but at the end of the day, it all falls back on me."

Manning worked with city officials to come to an agreement in 2006. "I ended up basically buying it from the city," Manning said. The decision ultimately saved the Miss Portland Diner. "They were like one step away from dumping this thing. I like a challenge, so I said let's do it."

The diner was moved to 140 Marginal Way, and a structure was built to attach it to. Manning reopened the Miss Portland Diner on October 31, 2008.

The life-changing decision, which Manning made with his wife, uprooted him from a longtime career at *Newsweek*. The risk—trading a corporate job in Manhattan for the difficult restaurant business—paid off. "It turned out. We're a pretty thriving business both for the tourists that come through [and the locals]," Manning said. "We have a huge local following. Our business doesn't dip down."

This blue diner with yellow lettering has seen the city grow and develop around it. Across the street, a pharmacy sits near a Trader Joe's and other stores. Next door, apartments were built. Manning said that the development of the area helped a little but not as much as it would have if the so-called Midtown Project was completed.

"It's been on the drawing board for seven years now," Manning said. A developer from Miami had four sixteen-story buildings planned to be built on Somerset. The project was approved by the city. "It basically would run from Whole Foods all the way to the back of Trader Joe's." However, a lawsuit derailed the project. The developer considered changes to the proposal, but the project lost momentum.

Nonetheless, Manning said that the Miss Portland gets steady business. "Our business goes up every year....We're in a very competitive market for restaurants, but our sales have gone up every year that we've been open," Manning said. He credits the cleanliness of the diner as part of its appeal. "We do a lot of the small things that I think restaurant owners don't want to spend the funds on."

The Miss Portland Diner also has a strong commitment to from-scratch cooking, something that was true of previous owners too. "I guess it was probably living and working in Manhattan, where there are really nice

An artist's rendering of the Miss Portland Diner hangs on the rear of the diner.

A list of local suppliers is seen in the Miss Portland Diner. The diner has a strong commitment to fresh, local, quality ingredients.

restaurants. I figured if it was worth doing, it was worth doing well....I take a lot of pride in the things that I do," Manning said. "I wanted to make it special. But in doing so, I also wanted to make it reasonably priced....We buy good product, and we make a lot of food from scratch. We buy most of our food from local vendors....We roast our own turkeys every day," Manning continued. "Our signature dish down there is the corned beef hash."

Manning, who said that despite his father owning a bar (Eddie's Shamrock Café), he really had no restaurant experience before buying the Miss Portland, provides oversite for the diner. He has experience now. "I'm there to make sure that things run smooth and run correctly. I help out back...I don't cook up on the line, but I can do everything else in the back," Manning said.

He likes to be visible to customers too. "Being from Portland, a lot of people that I knew or people that my family knew [come in]....People like to see the owner around," Manning said.

Before Manning bought the Miss Portland Diner, it had been closed for four years. "In the original diner car, it's all authentic, with the exception of the refrigeration," Manning said. And the historical commission in Portland kept a close eye on the development of the Miss Portland to be sure it stayed that way.

The Miss Portland Diner's signature corned beef hash is available on a benedict as well.

The efforts to keep the historic diner a thriving part of the community have been appreciated, Manning said. "It's something that brings back a lot of memories."

And it might just bring up some memories from film and television too. The Miss Portland Diner has made cameo appearances in films including *The Witch Files* and *Man Without a Face*.

The diner also gives back to its community in time and monetary support. Manning is on the board of the Boys and Girls Club, which he went to as a kid. The diner also sponsors Little League and Babe Ruth teams. "We're very visible in the community," Manning said. "I think that makes people feel good as well."

The Miss Portland Diner serves breakfast all day and has an extensive lunch and dinner menu. It also serves locally made cakes and pies.

With such a wide selection, it can be hard to choose a favorite, but Manning said he has one. "My favorite dish is probably the sausage and gravy on a southern biscuit," Manning said. The combination of the fluffy biscuit [with] the warm creamy sausage gravy is lovely.

How's the Corned Beef?

Excellent. No, really. The Miss Portland Diner offers its signature corned beef in omelets, in scrambles, on a benedict or on its own. Try them all. The corned beef features big pieces of shredded house-made corned beef with potatoes and carrots. It's delightful. Manning said that's probably the only recipe he's brought to the diner. Yes, it's his own.

Is Lobster on the Menu?

No.

Owner Favorite

Sausage and gravy on a southern biscuit.

How to Get There

Take exit 7 off Interstate-295. Turn right onto Marginal Way. Continue to Miss Portland Diner.

3

Modern Diners

Tourism, familiarity and good food at good prices: these are the things that have helped many diners—including new ones—thrive through the end of the twentieth century and into the twenty-first. Maine is, without a doubt, a different place today than it was ninety or so years ago, when diners first became popular here. But today's diners—both the classics and the new ones—offer a dose of nostalgia with every meal.

MAINE DINER

2265 Post Road, Wells
mainediner.com

When celebrity chef and *Diners, Drive-Ins, and Dives* star Guy Fieri was at the Maine Diner for a taping, he signed the wall. That signature stands, protected with a covering, above the kitchen door. A photo from the visit also hangs behind the counter.

There's also a blue neon Maine Diner clock and a print by photographer Liam Crotty. It's called *The Runaway* and is styled like Norman Rockwell's famed painting of the same name. It was shot at the counter of the Maine Diner, and print number four of one hundred hangs there.

The Maine Diner has been welcoming summer visitors and locals since 1983.

All of the waitresses wear different Maine Diner shirts. And from the counter to the booths, there's a general sense of welcoming and friendliness that permeates this diner.

Owner Jim MacNeill purchased the diner in 2018, after working there for years. He's the third owner since it opened in 1953. But time at the Maine Diner—as counted by its iconic status—didn't begin until the Henry brothers bought it in 1983. Dick and Myles Henry transformed the diner from a locals-only, off-season-only spot into the place it is today.

Socrates "Louie" Toton first opened what he called the Maine Restaurant in 1953. Toton was a Boston restaurateur, and the diner was his so-called retirement diner. He headed north for a slower pace and didn't want to deal with the influx of tourists who swell the population of Maine each summer. So, he didn't.

"Louie didn't open in the summer—he only opened in the winter. He hated tourists," MacNeill said. In the summertime, Toton cultivated a rich garden behind the building. Some of the produce would be sold at a farm stand. Today, pictures on the wall show that farm stand in the late 1950s, MacNeill said.

After Toton died, his sister sold the diner to the Henry brothers, who renamed it the Maine Diner and opened for business.

Behind the counter at the Maine Diner.

In a cookbook, *Maine Courses*, featuring the recipes of the Maine Diner, the Henry brothers wrote about how their first customer arrived by accident. "Literally by accident. He drove his car into a pole near our parking lot! It seems that he had mistaken us for a certain bar, and apparently zigged when he should have zagged," they wrote. That customer stayed for coffee and a meal and was one of forty-two who ate at the Maine Diner that day. The number of customers has grown—a lot—from there.

Toton's beloved garden is still behind the diner, and the produce is used in the restaurant today. It sits on about a half-acre behind the restaurant.

The Henry brothers took a different approach to running the diner than Toton, though. After buying it in February 1983, they began to build the

No, it's not a typo. The hamburg plate, a patty made of ground beef and served with gravy, is a diner favorite in Maine, including at the Maine Diner in Wells.

diner up as a destination spot for year-round diners. Customers responded, and the clientele of the diner slowly began to grow.

However, it was a few good mentions in the media that really helped the Maine Diner get on the travelers' map. "They caught a couple of good breaks in the late 1980s," MacNeill said.

Jane and Michael Stern, famed food writers who wrote the original *Roadfood* in 1978 (it's been revised at least seven times since then), included the Maine Diner in a revised version. When they were invited on the *Today* show to talk about a new edition of their book and their favorite spots in 1989, they included the Maine Diner. "Things exploded from there," MacNeill said.

In a 1998 article published in the *Portland Press Herald*, Myles Henry agreed. "It put us in a national light. It was initially overwhelming, but I'm extremely proud," Henry said.

The diner has been featured on Food Network's *Diners, Drive-Ins, and Dives*, the *Phantom Gourmet* and more. It's made more appearances on the *Today* show since then as well. It has also been mentioned in print media, including books, magazines and newspapers. The Sterns' companion website (roadfood.com) ranks the Maine Diner as "Legendary." Lonely Planet, the travel publisher, calls it "a step back in time, from decor to old-school menu."

"We got a ninety on the *Phantom Gourmet*, which I think we're the only diner ever to score a ninety or a ninety or better. Those are probably reserved for the more high-end restaurants," MacNeill said.

A Belgian waffle is seen at the Maine Diner. Corned beef hash can be seen in the background.

MacNeill has worked there on and off for twenty-one years, after being recruited by Myles Henry when he was working at a place down the street. MacNeill had a corporate job for a time and later went to school and ran a program at a community college while working part-time at the diner. About fifteen years ago, when the kitchen manager threw his keys down and walked out, MacNeill became the general manager and started working full time.

MacNeill's employment at the Maine Diner nearly ended in 2000, when popularity blew up thanks to the *Diners, Drive-Ins, and Dives* appearance. That was also the year the Henry brothers were awarded the Maine Restaurant Association's Restaurateur of the Year Award.

"With all those accolades, Myles wanted to take a more active role running the restaurant," MacNeill said. And while he understood this, MacNeill wanted his own place. It was time for a change and to move toward that goal, so he put in his notice and said he would remain until the annual winter shutdown began. (Every winter, the Maine Diner shuts down for a few weeks for upkeep and cleaning. It's a long-standing tradition that happens during the slow midwinter days.)

"I wasn't going to quit and leave them in a lurch," MacNeill said. Then everything changed. "And then December 5 of that year, Myles died. And he was actually the younger of the two brothers," MacNeill said. "Dicky got the call at 4:30 in the morning. Myles was on his [annual] Florida trip [with friends]....Dicky called me at 6:30 in the morning. I met him at the restaurant. I said, 'I'm not leaving now. You need me to stay. You need me more than you've ever needed me.'"

Myles Henry was only fifty-four years old. "Myles had a way of making customers feel special," his brother Todd told the *Portland Press Herald* after his death. "He made people want to come back again. It speaks volumes about the success of the business."

Plans were put on hold for both MacNeill, who had considered Myles Henry a mentor, and Dick Henry, who was sixty-two and nearing retirement.

"About five years ago, Dick and I started talking about me buying it when he was ready to retire," MacNeill said in 2019. "This year, he turned seventy and said it was time."

Effective June 29, 2018, MacNeill became the third owner in the eatery's history. "I call it change without change. If someone from the outside came in, they could have easily changed everything....A restaurant like this doesn't run like other restaurants," MacNeill said. And because of that, MacNeill didn't make a big deal out of the change in leadership. "I didn't want [concern] to spread because the same person that's been running it for eight years is the one who bought it."

The first waitress hired in 1983 still works there. In fact, the seniority list is so deep that MacNeill, who's worked there for more than two decades, isn't even close to the longest employee. "I am like eighteenth on the seniority list," MacNeill laughed. And that makes this diner different. The transient nature of the restaurant industry isn't the story of the Maine Diner, where MacNeill went three years without needing to hire a cook—a rarity.

"I feel we've always been very good to our employees," MacNeill said. "The staff, they're the bloodline to make sure the clientele receives what they expect to receive."

The food at the Maine Diner is classic diner with a twist. With a full breakfast menu, it has all the usual suspects, like corned beef hash, massive Belgian waffles and omelets, as well as dinner options like chicken pot pie and hot turkey sandwiches. It also has a robust menu of seafood dishes.

"One of our signature items is lobster pie," MacNeill said. The warm dish has a lot of lobster served with butter and lemon. If you order it, squeeze that lemon and dip your bites in the butter. It's a favorite of Jane and Michael Stern.

"The lobster roll is glorious, but the most amazing lobster dish, and one of the best regional dishes we've eaten anywhere, anytime, is the Henry brothers' grandmother's lobster pie. Of all the good Downeast things you

The Maine Diner's signature dish is the lobster pie, which is filled with sweet lobster chunks.

can eat along the coast, this casserole, elegant yet elementary, is one that mustn't be missed," the Sterns wrote on their website, roadfood.com.

The menu, which is large, can be a challenge in the winter, when storms can impact business. Still, MacNeill wants to provide the experience diners expect all year. "[As a diner,] you find something you like and you just have your heart set on having that, and if I were to go to a restaurant who said, 'We're running a condensed menu because it's winter,' I would be so pissed," MacNeill said. "Our job is to make every customer who walks through the door as happy as we possibly can because that will make them come back again."

And, he noted, though the menu is large, the ingredients are often used in several dishes. "The menu is huge, but there aren't a lot of things that are unique to one specific menu item," MacNeill said. "In the summertime, we go through stuff so fast. If we have a one hundred of something, we sell eighty."

For his part, MacNeill loves the "2s are wild" breakfast, which includes two eggs, two strips of bacon, two sausage links and two blueberry pancakes with toast. "Our blueberry pancakes—nobody can touch them. They are the best ever," MacNeill said. He also loves the fried food on the menu—especially the clams and scallops.

There's been a lot of good attention on the diner lately, including a mention in a *Yankee* magazine online story. "It blew up on Facebook. It absolutely blew up on Facebook, and then I had people up the wazoo congratulating me," MacNeill said.

It's not just the staff who have longevity with the diner; it's the diners too. "We watched a lot of people grow up," MacNeill said. "Like the Cohens—I have watched their kids grow up. Now they come in, and they have kids," MacNeill said. "I've known a kid since he was twelve, and all of the sudden, he's coming in with his children. And we've watched people pass away. We've built so many relationships with so many people and that's part of, to me, the character of the diner."

So are the regulars, who have favorite tables and traditions. "We have a group of women called the 'Walkers,' and they walk up from Drake's Island every morning and sit down and have coffee," MacNeill said. The staff looks forward to chatting with them.

There's also a group of locals who come in every morning and sit at counter seats one through four. "They will all slide down if one has to leave. And if one of them is late and someone else takes their seat, it's like mayhem. They will sit at one of the middle tables, and they will glare at them until they leave, and as soon as they leave, they will get up and take the seat," MacNeill said.

From teachers to families, the regulars are an important part of the diner. "We take the time to get to know these people. We recognize people, and we want to get to know them, and that's one of the things that sets us apart," MacNeill said.

In 1998, Myles Henry told the *Portland Press Herald* that the secret to the diner's success was how the staff treated customers—a commitment that continues to this day. "Our biggest thing is to try to treat guests like they're in our own home," Myles Henry said. "I really think that's what we do well."

Even though the Henry brothers no longer own the Maine Diner, their guiding touch remains everywhere in the beloved diner, including on the menu and logo, which was drawn by their brother Bruce.

How Is the Corned Beef Hash?

It's your standard corned beef hash and is perfectly good. But with such a robust menu, be more adventurous. The she-crab soup is delightful and packed with crab. And the lobster pie is wonderful.

Is Lobster on the Menu?

Oh, yes, and the Maine Diner has been praised for it. There's the beloved lobster pie, plus a lobster roll, lobster salad, lobster mac and cheese, lobster quiche and lobster club.

Owner Favorite

MacNeill has many, but he particularly loves the blueberry pancakes.

How to Get There

Take exit 25 off Interstate 95. Continue to Alewive Park Road, and then turn left onto Alewive Road. Turn left on to ME-35 South (Fletcher Street). At the traffic circle, take the first exit onto Storer Street. Turn right onto US-1 South (York Street). Follow for a little over three miles. The diner will be on your left.

BECKY'S DINER

390 Commercial Street, Portland
www.beckysdiner.com

Set in the Old Port just off the wharf, Becky's Diner is housed in a quaint New England building. With long hours and excellent food, it draws crowds all year long. On warm days, you can smell the wharf outside.

Step through the doors of this busy diner, and you're transported. Take it all in—the faux wood tile floor, the honey colored wood creeping up the walls. The off-white tin ceilings are beautiful. The red pleather stools at the counter welcome diners. Matching red booths greet larger parties and families. It's the details that make the interior of this larger diner so interesting. A window opens between the two sides of the restaurant. There are ceramic curtains around the window and a small mirror. Matching ceramic pots filled with plants line the windowsills. Care has been taken in creating the experience here.

Becky's Diner, a Portland favorite, is located near the wharf.

The pancakes are fluffy and soft, sweetened to a pleasant flavor. The omelets are generous, with folds of thin, perfectly cooked egg concealing the fillings within. Breakfast is served all day and night.

Becky's Diner opened in March 1991, serving breakfast and lunch. It later expanded to offer dinner as well. "Say a guy's covered with grease and he wants to eat," Becky Rand told the *Portland Press Herald* in 1995. "There's nowhere to get any food on the waterfront unless he wants to drive to McDonald's. All the [other] restaurants are too nice. I'm not trying to be a nice restaurant."

According to a 2016 article by the weekly newspaper the *Forecaster*, Rand "mortgaged her home to open a diner in a once boarded-up building." The divorced mother of six had been working in several restaurants to make ends meet. She saw an opportunity in the one-story building and grabbed it, leasing the building from its owners—ten fishermen and a lawyer.

"I thought I was just going to be a little coffee shop. To get on this side of the street, I had to sell food to the fishermen," Rand told the *Forecaster*.

She's referring to a 1987 ordinance, approved by vote in Portland, that restricted which businesses could operate on that side of Commercial Street

An inside look at Becky's Diner.

to only those related to marine uses. The aim was to preserve Portland's so-called working waterfront. Rand's diner fit the bill because she catered for fishing events and sold food to the fisherman.

"They were super-kind landlords who made it possible for me to succeed," she told the *Forecaster*.

As Rand's business grew, so did the need for more space. However, the 1987 ordinance prevented expansion unless she could get city approval from the Portland Planning Board. Seeking to build a second story and expand the kitchen, increasing the overall blueprint to about 2,700 square feet, Rand asked the city for an exception to the code.

"The issue I'm wrestling with is how to gauge the impact on marine uses," board member David Silk told the *Portland Press Herald* at the time. He and other board members were concerned about unintended consequences.

Although she was understanding—Rand too wanted to preserve the working waterfront—she was adamant about the need. "There's a need to feed this group of people who are working on the waterfront," Rand told the *Portland Press Herald*. "A guy who is cutting fish, he doesn't want to go up and sit in one of those cafes in the Old Port. If it were about money, I'd get a liquor license."

The expansion was ultimately permitted with a zoning text change, according to an October 2005 article in the *Portland Press Herald*. In 2007, the diner underwent a large renovation. "With our loyal customers' understanding, we were able to remain open throughout this construction project. We are now able to offer more inside seating, outside porch seating overlooking Portland's waterfront, and a meeting room for larger groups," Rand wrote on the diner's website.

The diner is a beloved local institution. In 2012, the *Portland Press Herald* wrote, "Becky's is a lively, bustling place on the waterfront, so you see different kinds of folks, from lobstermen and waterfront workers to tourists, teens and entire families." This is a family-run diner that has employed all of Rand's six children, along with some nieces and nephews over the years.

Becky's is a place that caters to locals but attracts a strong tourist market too. It's also a hotspot for visiting politicians and candidates on the campaign trail, as well as their famous supporters. Other famous people in town for concerts, performances and tapings also stop there, just because. Moreover, this beloved spot has garnered much media attention over the years. It's been featured on Food Network's *Diners, Drive-Ins, and Dives* and has been mentioned in dozens of top publications as a must-try.

Left: Becky's Diner serves classic diner fare, including stuffed omelets, like the broccoli and cheese pictured here. In the background, you can see Becky's house-made corned beef hash. It's excellent.

Below: Customers sit at the counter at Becky's Diner on a spring day in 2018.

In October 1999, *Gourmet* magazine—then a bastion of the best dining in the world—praised Becky's Diner: "If you're still a little tired as the day begins, walking into Becky's is a friendly thanks-I-needed that slap in the face. You have entered nothing short of diner heaven."

In 2014, *Condé Nast Traveler* included Becky's Diner in its story "10 Most Popular US Diners," writing, "Make sure you don't miss the popular blueberry pancakes, lobster and swiss omelette, or the homemade corn beef hash."

In 2015, Eater Maine named Becky's one of its "24 Classic Restaurants Every Mainer Must Try." In 2018, Delish.com named it one of "The Absolute Best Restaurants in Portland, Maine," writing, "The fact that it's fast, cheap, and on the water are not the only reasons to start your day at this Portland establishment: Chefs here also have blueberry pancakes that will raise your pancake bar 4 lyfe."

In 2016, the *New York Times* included Becky's in its "36 Hours in Portland, ME," feature. It recommended Becky's for Sunday breakfast, suggesting buttermilk pancakes, eggs and home fries, and writing, "Expect a modest check and the satisfaction that you've experienced a Portland classic." *Cosmopolitan* even named it the cutest diner in Maine in 2017.

But at its heart, Becky remains that special spot dedicated to the working waterfront, where fishermen and lobstermen can get a hot bite at 4:00 a.m. It's friendly and warm, as so many reporters have noted over the years. But it's also good, honest food served at good prices. Is it any wonder so many people love Becky's?

How Is the Corned Beef Hash?

Is there a stronger word than excellent? The house-made corned beef hash at Becky's Diner is exquisite. It's perfection. It's all good things. Shredded corned beef mingles with big chunks of potatoes and carrots in this well-seasoned dish. If you like corned beef, order it here, but make sure you ask for the homemade hash. They also serve the canned version, but you don't want that one.

Is Lobster on the Menu?

Yes. There's a lobster and Swiss omelet, a lobster roll, a lobster salad bowl and whole lobsters. Becky's Diner has a lobster tank, so when you order lobster, it's really fresh.

How to Get There:
Take exit 6A off Interstate 295. Merge onto Forest Avenue. Turn right onto State Street. Continue for about a mile. Turn left onto York Street and then right onto High Street. Turn left onto Commercial Street. The diner will be on your right. There's street parking and some parking in the lot, but respect the signs, as some of the parking is reserved for other businesses.

NICKY'S CRUISIN' DINER

957 Union Street, Bangor
nickyscruisindiner.com

A former ice cream shop turned diner, Nicky's Cruisin' Diner is an ode to the '50s and '60s. In the larger dining room, a wall of license plates is fascinating to look at. Pop culture paraphernalia featuring Marilyn Monroe, Elvis and the Beatles, as well as a jukebox and a guitar decorate the room. With its black and white checkerboard flooring and white wainscoting, it's fun.

Nicky's Cruisin' Diner is owned by Howie and Karen Day, who met while Howie was working at the ice cream shop under the former owners. The Days married in 1985.

"Then [in] November of 1987, the owner of the business at that time offered to sell to us. He and his wife owned another restaurant at that time. So, we bought it," Karen Day said. "We knew from the time we were dating to married that we really wanted to own a business."

The days continued to run the business as Nicky's Ice Cream Parlor until the mid-1990s. "We legally changed the name to Nicky's Crusin' Diner around 1994," Karen Day said. The first cruise night was held in the summer of 1993. Cruise nights are now held every Wednesday night from May to September.

"When we took over Nicky's, the restaurant had five booths and a long counter with stools. In 1994, we removed the counter and stools and added the booths to make more seating available in the front, then in 1996, we added the back dining room," Karen Day said.

The diner has hosted a number of notable guests over the years. When President Barack Obama was first campaigning, he made a visit to Nicky's. Stephen King, a Bangor resident, has had "many visits" at Nicky's with

Nicky's Cruisin' Diner is a local favorite.

friends, family and business associates, Karen Day said. It's even been the site of a wedding proposal and a wedding day.

But it's the regulars who give the diner a rhythm. "We could paper a room with photos of all the regulars we have had over the last thirty years," Karen Day said. "They hang out drinking coffee two, three, maybe four times a day. They share in the exciting times and stressful times of the staff and of each other. We have ideas of what they will have for breakfast, lunch or dinner, depending on the day and time."

The relationships forged go beyond the ordering process. At Nicky's, the staff and the regulars are considered an extension of the Day family. "You worry when you don't see them. We mourn their deaths. We joke, we laugh, and we will argue too," Karen Day said. "It is a blessing and can be a curse all at the same time. Sometimes a person visiting Nicky's for the first time may be put off by how we interact with a regular customer. But that is what makes Nicky's Nicky's."

Those regulars aren't just locals—they include travelers who pass through Bangor. Everyone is welcome at this familiar spot. "You can stop in at lunchtime and see a table of young parents with their children, a group of retires having lunch, a group of military [personnel], a group of business people from nearby, sports teams from little league to college teams and just about anyone else," Karen Day said.

Nicky's has grown over the years. "When we took over Nicky's, the restaurant had five booths and a long counter with stools. In 1994, we

The sign at Nicky's Cruisin' Diner welcomes hungry patrons and classic car enthusiasts.

Among the owners' favorites: the Philly steak and cheese wrap at Nicky's Cruisin' Diner in Bangor.

removed the counter and stools and added the booths to make more seating available in the front, then in 1996 we added the back dining room," Karen Day said.

For the Days, the greatest challenge is finding dedicated, hardworking, fun, polite, trustworthy employees. "Our core staff have been with us for many, many years and are a huge reason for our continued success. They understand the importance of teamwork and how all the parts, from the cook to the servers to the cashier to the dishwasher, make a good impression and enjoyable visit," Karen Day said

Over the last thirty years, the Days have seen the diner business change and adapt to altering desires of customers. Customers today, Day said, want a more personalized experience. "Being able to add or delete an item from an omelet or sandwich, having a wide variety of sides to choose from for your meal, that willingness to make substitutions—within reason—makes for a more enjoyable experience," Karen Day said.

The growth of diagnosed food allergies has also changed how they operate, but the Days do their best to accommodate. "When we first took over Nicky's, a customer could choose from French fries, onion rings or coleslaw for a side. And you just didn't hear about or think about diet fads or dietary allergies/restrictions," Karen Day said.

Nicky's Cruisin' Diner serves a reliable list of breakfast favorites all day. When asked about their favorite dishes, the Days couldn't choose just one.

A diner classic, the breakfast tray features pancakes, eggs, baked beans and more at Nicky's Cruisin' Diner.

Seen through the front window, this portion of Nicky's Cruisin' Diner is part of the original restaurant, which was initially an ice cream shop.

The back room at Nicky's Cruisin' Diner features memorabilia, including license plates.

"Howie enjoys fried scallops or fried haddock, Philly ciabatta sandwich or Philly wrap, chicken Caesar salad or wrap, mac and cheese, chicken tenders, all breakfast—he really likes breakfast—cheeseburgers, super quesadilla with grilled chicken," Karen Day said.

For her favorites, she also listed many, including fried shrimp. "I prefer breakfast for dinner, and I would go raisin bread French toast or eggs benedict [with] sauce on side. I'm not much for sauce or gravy," Karen Day said.

They also both like the hot turkey and hot pot roast sandwiches. "As you can tell, we don't have a favorite," Karen Day said.

How Is the Corned Beef Hash?

For those who love standard diner fare corned beef, Nicky's Cruisin' Diner delivers with a generous portion of corned beef with soft and crispy parts. But their eggs benedict are truly special, with a tangy hollandaise sauce that's just delightful.

CLASSIC DINERS OF MAINE

Is Lobster on the Menu?
No.

Owner Favorite
Too many to list.

How to Get There
From I-95, take exit 184 for Union Street. If coming from the north, turn right onto Union Street. If coming from the south, turn left. Follow Union Street to your destination. Nicky's Cruisin' Diner will be on your right.

4

More Noteworthy Diners

With so many establishments from border to border calling themselves diners, I wanted to call attention to a few more noteworthy ones. Some of these are housed in true diners, while others have a special history and still others just have excellent diner food.

BLAST FROM THE PAST

114 Sokokis Trail East, Waterboro
blastfromthepastme.com

A 1950-style diner serving handmade food like your mom might have served—if she cooked. Think classics like meatloaf, American chop suey and pot roast, along with diner essentials like pancakes and corned beef hash.

What Makes It Notable

This is a Valiant Diners modular diner built in Ormond Beach, Florida. It was shipped to Maine in three pieces and opened in July 2004. The diner hosts cruise nights on Friday evenings from mid-May to mid-September. Its sister diner, Blast from the Past Too, is located at 623 US-1 in Scarborough. Although that has a similar look, a 2007 article in the *Portland Press Herald* indicates that it was build on-site. Original owner

Mike Glaude went for a 1950s style in stainless steel, with neon lights and cherry red leather. It was initially opened as the Rock 'n' Roll Diner but was later purchased by the family behind the Blast from the Past diner, and its name was changed.

DAVE'S DINER

390 Brunswick Avenue, Gardiner

Not far from the interstate, this is a popular stop for both locals and travelers. Expect diner classics, including big Belgium waffles, perfectly cooked eggs and an amazing eggs Benedict.

What Makes It Notable
According to the Kansas Historical Society, Dave's Diner is a Valentine Diners double deluxe that opened in 1965 as Pat's Diner. Valentine Diners were built in Kansas. The staff is excellent, and the food is too.

DENNY'S DINER

123 Civic Center Drive, Augusta
120 Haskell Road, Bangor

The national chain has invested in real diners at some locations. Two operate in Maine and serve standard Denny's fare, including pancakes, French toast and sandwiches.

What Makes Them Notable
Opened in 1999, both of these are Starlite Diners built in in Ormond, Florida. The company creates shiny silver, modular 1950s-style diners.

Martha's Diner in Ellsworth might be located in a strip mall, but it's the real diner experience.

Denny's Diner in Bangor, Maine, is among several Starlite Diners in the state.

DOWNTOWN DINER

204 Water Street, Augusta

Open for breakfast and lunch, Downtown Diner has a menu of classics from omelets and egg plates to pancakes and waffles. For lunch, the selections include a variety of burgers and sandwiches.

What Makes It Notable
This sweet storefront diner is located in a historic building in downtown Augusta. The location was the home of Hersey's Shoe Store. Inside, you'll find a welcoming staff and comfortable environment. The menu is great too.

FARMINGTON D

367 Wilton Road, Farmington
farmingtond.com

Open for breakfast, lunch and dinner, this diner is located in the building that formerly housed Harvest House Restaurant. Opened in late 2018, it serves diner classics.

What Makes It Notable
The owner of this diner, Rachel Jackson, owns the dining car that was the Farmington Diner. Keep an eye on this one. She's said in multiple interviews that she would love to have the Farmington Diner return to service someday. Regarding the name, Jackson told the *Livermore Falls Advertiser* in August 2018, "The name Farmington D…is like a game of Hangman. We can fill in the word 'diner' when it comes time."

LITTLE RED HEN DINER & BAKERY

28 South Main Street, Andover
littleredhendiner.com

A partial menu on its website reveals the usual diner suspects for breakfast (including three options for eggs benedict), along with an array of sandwiches, wraps and burgers for lunch. This diner opens for dinner on some nights, including their Prime Rib Fridays. It is a favorite among hikers.

What Makes It Notable

Good karma. This family-run diner draws rave reviews from customers for its simple, homestyle diner food. But what's special is how they give back to the world at large. They are very hiker-friendly and allow thru-hikers on the Appalachian Trail to camp in a field behind the diner.

MARCY'S DINER

47 Oak Street, Portland

Originally opened in 1941, Marcy's Diner has had a number of owners over the years. It serves classic diner fare at reasonable prices. This is a cash-only establishment.

What Makes It Notable

Marcy's Diner is known for its diner classics and loyal following. It made national headlines in 2015, when owner Darla Neugebauer clashed with a family whose toddler had been crying for a while. Neugebauer yelled at the child to be quiet. The mother of the child left a negative review on the Marcy's Diner Facebook page, and a national debate ensued over the diner owner's rights versus the guest's rights.

MARTHA'S DINER

151 High Street #7, Ellsworth
marthasdiner.com/

Open for breakfast and lunch most days, this is a cozy diner in an unexpected place. Its menu is filled with omelets with local place names. (What does it say about the Queen City that the Bangor omelet is a plain two egg omelet?) The waitstaff is personable, and the specials are worth considering.

Above: Martha's Diner in Ellsworth serves up classic diner fare at good prices.

Left: Inside Martha's Diner in Ellsworth.

What Makes It Notable

Don't be fooled by the strip mall location. Martha's diner serves fresh, wholesome, delicious diner food in a fun, '50s-themed space. Try the eggs benedict. And don't forget the cash, as it is cash-only.

The Miss Wiscasset Diner is located on Route 1 in Wiscasset.

MISS WISCASSET DINER

762 Bath Road, Wiscasset

An adorable little red diner on Route 1, the Miss Wiscasset Diner serves diner classics from pancakes and eggs to a house-made corned beef hash that some internet reviewers call the best they've ever had.

What Makes It Notable
Originally opened in the 1960s, this red roadside dinner is beloved and open year-round.

Q STREET DINER

9 Q Street, South Portland
qstreetdiner.com

Inside this friendly diner, newer black booths line one room where vintage concert posters and ads for Pennzoil Motor Oil and Gargoyle Motor Oil

The Q Street Diner is located in South Portland.

The sign for the Q Street Diner is seen from the road.

(a bargain at thirty cents) line the walls. This cash-only diner is clean and eager to please.

What Makes It Notable

This funky classic diner is friendly and serves up classic diner fare at good prices. Try their fluffy pancakes.

UNCLE ANDY'S DINER

171 Ocean Street, South Portland
uncleandysdiner.com

Alongside the diner classics here, you can find a special seasonal omelet called the lobsterman omelette. It comes filled with lobster meat, fresh corn, tomato and cheddar cheese and is served with home fries and toast.

What Makes It Notable

Uncle Andy's has been feeding customers in South Portland since 1954. It was featured on Food Network's *Restaurant Impossible* in 2014.

WACO DINER

47 Water Street, Eastport

Breakfast is served all day here, and it's open year-round. Perhaps the best time to visit is in the summertime, when you can sit on the patio and dine al fresco on the water.

What Makes It Notable

The WaCo Diner began its life in 1924 as a lunch cart. Named for its original owners, Nelson Watts and Ralph Colwell, it's on the water in Eastport—a lovely location.

5

A Partial Timeline of Maine Diner History

From the days of lunch carts to the rise of dining cars to the present, when diners exist in a variety of buildings, diners in Maine have offered reliable, affordable food to locals and travelers alike. This is a partial timeline of Maine diner history.

1924: WaCo Diner opens as a lunch cart in Eastport, Maine.

1927: Palace Diner is opened in Biddeford by Louis Lachance and Orville Pollard. It was one of the few Pollard Diners made in Lowell, Massachusetts.

1928: Deluxe Diner opens in Rumford. The Worcester Lunch Car Company dining car was taken by rail to Rumford and then moved to its location using a team of horses. The car was placed above a hand-dug cellar. It's not clear what name the diner went by at this time.

Mid-1930s: The Miss Brunswick Diner opens in Brunswick. Owned by Alcide Thibeault, this diner has no relation to the modern Miss Brunswick Diner.

1934: When the new Route 1 opens, the lunch cart that the Moodys run is there with a porch added on. This is the first iteration of Moody's Diner.

1937: Bridge Street Lunch opens in Gardiner, Maine.

1939: Local horse trainer and driver C. Pierce Chappelle of Lewiston has the Norway Diner built in Norway, Maine. It has a barrel roof, like popular dining car–style buildings at the time.

1940: The Norway Diner opens in Norway, Maine.

1946: Heald's Diner opens in Gardiner, Maine. It replaces Bridge Street Lunch. It is Worcester Lunch Car Company diner No. 790.

1948: The Norway Diner moves to 101.5 Pleasant Street in Brunswick, Maine. It is renamed the Norwago Diner.

The Miss Portland Diner.

1949: The Norwago Diner in Brunswick, Maine, is opened by new owner Robert Buchanan.

The Miss Portland Diner opens at 175 Forest Avenue. It is Worcester Lunch Car Company dining car No. 818 and is owned by Jimmie Crowder Jr.

Moody's Diner expands, moving the back wall of the kitchen out five feet. The construction happens overnight, with the diner staff cooking in the new space the next morning.

1952: Maurice Wakefield buys Heald's Diner. The name is changed to Wakefield's.

1953: The Miss Brunswick Diner is torn down. A store is to replace it.

Boston restauranteur Socrates "Louie" Toton buys the land and building that will eventually become the Maine Diner. He runs the restaurant seasonally—closed all summer—and has an extensive garden behind it. He calls it the Maine Restaurant.

1954: Uncle Andy's Diner opens in South Portland.

1960s: Miss Wiscasset Diner opens.

Farmington Diner reportedly opens in Farmington, Maine. It is a Mountain View diner that was built in 1949.

1962: Palace Diner is sold to Roland Beaudoin.

1964: The Miss Portland Diner moves to 49 Marginal Way. It's now owned by Harold Foley and Albert Karas.

1964–66: Raynald "Pete" Beaudoin takes over the Palace Diner from his father.

1965: Pat's Diner opens in Gardiner, Maine. It is a Valentine Diners double deluxe. In 2020, it is known as Dave's Diner.

1971: The Wirebridge Diner opens in New Portland, Maine. It is Worcester Lunch Car Company dining car No. 698 and was built in 1932. It's unclear when it closed, but it was sometime after 2004.

1972: The Norwago Diner is renamed the "Miss Brunswick Diner" by owner Ed Buckley. It appears as the Miss Brunswick Diner in the Brunswick directory for the first time in 1975.

1979: Albert and Elizabeth Giberson buy Wakefield's in Gardiner, Maine. They rename it the Giberson Diner.

1980s: The Minute Man Diner opens in Springfield, Maine. It is Worcester Lunch Car Company dining car No. 649 and was built in 1929. By 2004, it was closed and abandoned.

The A1 Diner.

1981: Randall Chasse buys the Miss Portland Diner.

1983: Dick and Myles Henry purchase the Maine Restaurant. They rename it the Maine Diner.

1986: Larry B. and Fay Ann Smith buy the Miss Brunswick Diner.

1987: Michael Giberson and his partner, Neil Anderson, purchase the Giberson Diner in Gardiner, Maine, from Giberson's parents. They rename it the A1 Diner.

Howie and Karen Day buy Nicky's Ice Cream Parlor in Bangor, Maine.

1989: The Maine Diner is mentioned by food writers Jane and Michael Stern in a segment on the *Today* show. It sparks an explosion of business for the diner.

1991: Becky's Diner opens in the Old Port in Portland, Maine.

1994: Randall Chasse tries to sell the Miss Portland Diner through an essay contest. Not enough entries are received.

1994–95: Moody's Diner expands again, extending the restaurant and raising the roof. It was also rewired, and new duct work was installed to improve the heating and cooling.

Mid-1990s: Andre and Cathleen Prest buy the Miss Brunswick Diner.

Becky's Diner.

Nicky's Ice Cream Parlor becomes Nicky's Cruisin' Diner in Bangor, Maine.

1993: Nicky's Cruisin' Diner in Bangor begins holding seasonal "cruise nights."

1996: Jane Davis buys the Miss Brunswick Diner.

Nicky's Cruisin' Diner expands, adding a back dining room.

Raynald "Pete" Beaudoin retires. Tony Ouellette takes over the Palace Diner under a lease with the option to buy agreement. The deal falls through, and the diner closes six weeks later.

1997: Rick and Joanne Bernier purchase and reopen the Palace Diner.

1999: National chain Denny's opens two new locations in Maine. Both the Bangor and Augusta locations are Starlite Diners built by the Modular Diner company in Ormond, Florida.

2000: Moody's Diner ends its twenty-four-hour service.

The Maine Diner appears on *Diners, Drive-Ins, and Dives*. Owners Myles and Dick Henry are awarded the Maine Restaurant Association's Restaurateur of the Year Award. Myles Henry dies unexpectedly in December.

The Maine Diner.

2001: Randall Chasse tries to sell the Miss Portland Diner by eBay auction. No bids are received.

2004: The Miss Portland Diner closes. Randall Chasse sells the land to a developer and donates the dining car to the City of Portland.

2005: Blast from the Past diner opens in East Waterboro. It's a Valiant modular diner that was built in Ormond Beach, Florida.

Kyle and Debbie Quinn purchase the Palace Diner.

2006: Tom Manning reaches an agreement to purchase the Miss Portland Diner from the City of Portland.

2007: Becky's Diner expands, adding more dining space and a second story. The kitchen is expanded as well.

Farmington Diner closes. The building is bought and moved to private property.

2008: The Miss Portland Diner reopens at 140 Marginal Way in Portland.

2011: The Capotosto family purchases the Palace Diner.

2013: The Palace Diner closes on August 31. Later that year, in November, Chad Conley and Greg Mitchell sign an agreement to lease the diner with an option to buy.

2014: Jodi Campbell and Julie Kiley purchase the Deluxe Diner from Connie Arsenault.

2018: Restaurant manager Jim MacNeill buys the Maine Diner from Dick Henry. He plans to keep everything the same and tries to keep the change of ownership quiet.

Aaron Harris buys the A1 Diner. For the first time in the diner's history, the new owner doesn't change the diner's name.

6

Dining Car Companies

Since the late 1800s, dozens and dozens of companies have manufactured structures meant for quick meals, beginning with the lunch carts of the late 1800s. T.H. Buckley of Worcester, Massachusetts, was particularly well known for his lunch carts that were manufactured in a factory at 281 Grafton Street from 1891 until 1908. Lunch carts were popular in those days in Maine as well.

In the early 1900s in Bangor, for instance, lunch carts were licensed by the city each spring. "Lunch carts at busy street corners were a common sight. They sold hot dogs and other delicacies even well after dark to men working the night shift, movie goers and holiday revelers," wrote history columnist Wayne E. Reilly in a 2014 column for the *Bangor Daily News*.

Lunch carts appeared in Portland, Bath and other Maine cities. Then a new generation of similar businesses arose in the form of the more permanent dining car diners. Workers could stop in, sit down and have a swift meal at a working-man's price. The concept caught on, and soon, there were diners near many of Maine's mills.

The following are some of the companies that created prefabricated structures for diners in Maine.

WORCESTER LUNCH CAR COMPANY

The Worcester Lunch Car Company was founded in 1906 by Philip Duprey and Irving Stoddard. They manufactured lunch cars based on the railroad dining car at a factory in Worcester, Massachusetts. Those early diners were built to serve late night customers from factories, according to the Worcester Historical Museum. They were desirable because they came ready to cook and were easily moved.

The lunch cars were built to order and featured porcelain exteriors, often emblazoned with the diner's name in an intricate font. They also featured oak and mahogany interiors, counter seating and tile floors.

A number of Worcester Lunch Car diners came to operate in Maine. The Minute Man Diner, for instance, was Worcester Lunch Car Company No. 649 and was built in 1929. It was initially installed in Lynn, Massachusetts, but moved several times before ending up in Springfield, Maine, in the 1980s. It's closed now.

The Wirebridge Diner in New Portland, Maine, was also a Worchester diner. It is Worcester Lunch Car Company No. 698. Originally located in Waterville, it moved to New Portland in 1971. It closed sometime after 2004.

Others, like the Miss Portland Diner, continue to operate here.

The Worcester Lunch Car Company closed in 1961, after crafting 651 diners.

Remaining WLCC Diners in Maine

Deluxe Diner (1928)
29 Oxford Avenue, Rumford
No. unknown

A1 Diner (1946)
3 Bridge Street, Gardiner
No. 790

Miss Portland Diner (1949)
140 Marginal Way, Portland
No. 818

THE POLLARD COMPANY

The Pollard Company of Lowell, Massachusetts, was one of many companies that manufactured lunch cars in the early to mid-twentieth century. It was only in operation for two years, from 1926 to 1927, but there are two known dining cars from the Pollard Company still in use.

The Bristol Diner in Bristol, New Hampshire, is set in a larger building, giving it a larger blueprint. The other remaining Pollard diner is the Palace Diner in Biddeford, Maine. First owners Louis Lachance of Kennebunk and his brother-in-law Orville Pollard brought it from the assembly line in Lowell to Biddeford, where it served a hungry crowd from nearby mills.

Lachance, it's said, worked at the Pollard Company factory, and Pollard was part of the family that operated the manufacturer.

Remaining Pollard Company Diners in Maine

Palace Diner (1927)
18 Franklin Street, Biddeford

MOUNTAIN VIEW DINERS

From 1939 to 1957, Mountain View Diners was operated in Singac, New Jersey, by owners Les Daniel and Henry Strys. The company was known for creating quality-manufactured, on-trend diners for eager restaurateurs.

One of those diners, a 1949 model, made its way north to Farmington in the 1960s, where it served the hungry college community until 2007, when it closed.

There are no remaining Mountain View Diners operating in Maine, but the closed Farmington Diner is privately owned and still resides in the Pine Tree State on private property. Its owner, who opened the Farmington D in 2018, hopes to get it up and running in Farmington in the future.

VALIANT STARLITE DINERS

Previously known as Starlite Diners, Valiant Starlite Diners in Ormond Beach, Florida, is a modern manufacturer of modular diners that are characterized by their shiny stainless-steel exteriors. Created in 1992, this company is family owned and makes made-to-order, fully customizable diners. Its units have been used across the United States and abroad, including in Russia and Germany.

Valiant Starlite Diners in Maine:

Blast from the Past
114 Sokokis Trail, East Waterboro

Denny's Diner
123 Civic Center Drive, Augusta
120 Haskell Road, Bangor

7
Diner Cooking at Home

Diners are wonderful to visit. There's so much atmosphere, personality and delight in having someone make an amazing meal for you. But sometimes you want that diner food experience without having to leave the comfort of your home. The following recipes are designed for those times. These easy recipes from my own repertoire will help you create the diner experience in your own kitchen. Enjoy!

PROGRESSIVE RECIPES

Diners often make multiple dishes using the same base ingredients. Sometimes this means cooking a turkey to make several dishes or keeping freshly made corned beef on hand. This allows them to offer more options on the menu while not adding ingredients that can only be used for a few. The following recipes build on each other, allowing you to repurpose and reuse foods in different ways.

Slow Cooker Corned Beef
Serves 4 to 6
Prep time: 5 minutes
Cook time: 10 hours

Several recipes in this book call for corned beef. This easy method makes it fall apart tender and perfect for sandwiches, hash and more. You could, of course, serve this as dinner, but this recipe is intended to provide corned beef for other recipes.

1 corned beef brisket (2 to 3 pounds) with seasoning packet (flat cut preferred)
1 bay leaf

Rinse the corned beef thoroughly under cool water. Place in the slow cooker and cover with water. The water should rise at least an inch higher than the corned beef. Sprinkle the seasoning packet into the slow cooker. Add the bay leaf. Cover and cook on low for 10 hours. Remove the corned beef from the slow cooker. Let sit for 10 minutes before slicing against the grain.

Cooking tip: No seasoning packet? No problem. Throw in a few whole peppercorns, allspice berries and mustard seeds, along with a sprinkling of salt and pepper. Cook as directed above.

Homemade Corned Beef Hash
Serves 4
Prep time: 10 minutes
Cook time: 20 minutes

Inspired by the fine house-made corned beef hash at the Miss Portland Diner and Becky's Diner, this recipe is loaded with big bits of shredded corned beef, potatoes and carrots. Delightful with fried or poached eggs, this is a satisfying breakfast.

2 tablespoons olive oil, divided
1 small onion, quartered and sliced (about ¼-inch-thick slices)
8 ounces (½ pound) prepared corned beef, shredded (2 cups)
1¼ cups boiled potatoes, diced
½ cup boiled carrots, diced

Heat 1 tablespoon olive oil in a large skillet over medium heat. Add the onions and cook, stirring occasionally, until golden—about 7 to 10 minutes. Add 1 tablespoon olive oil to the skillet along with the corned beef, potatoes and carrots. Stir. Season with salt and pepper. Cook, stirring infrequently, for 8 to 10 minutes, until cooked through. There should be browned sections mixed in.

Cooking tip: This is best made with leftovers. When you are making corned beef, choose a slightly larger piece so you'll have about a half pound left over to make this too.

Pressed Reuben Sandwich
Serves 4

The Reuben is a classic diner sandwich and a personal favorite. Best made with fresh corned beef (don't give in to the luncheon meat), it's delightful with or without dressing or mustard.

olive oil
8 slices marble rye bread
12 ounces cooked corned beef, sliced
about 1 cup sauerkraut
4 slices (1 ounce each) Swiss cheese
Thousand Island dressing or spicy mustard (optional)

For this recipe, you need either a grill pan with a press or a grill appliance (like the George Foreman Grill). See tip at end of recipe for an alternative method if you don't have those.

Preheat the grill pan and press (or grill appliance) over medium heat. Brush one side of each slice of bread with olive oil. Once the pan is hot, remove the press and place one slice of bread, olive oil side down, in the pan. Top with corned beef, sauerkraut and cheese. If using dressing or spicy mustard, brush on the untouched side of another slice of bread, and then top the sandwich with it. Press the sandwich down and grill, flipping once, until toasted and browned, about 5 to 7 minutes total. Repeat until all sandwiches have been made. Cut in half and enjoy.

Cooking tip: For an unpressed version of this sandwich, omit the olive oil and instead butter one side of each slice of bread. Prepare and cook as directed above, placing the butter side down in the pan. Don't press it down but do flip the sandwich after 2 to 3 minutes. Cook until browned on both sides.

Buttermilk Biscuits
Yields 9 biscuits
Prep time: 15 minutes
Cook time: 16 minutes

Tender and flaky, these biscuits rise as they cook. Delicious hot from the oven, they are also wonderful warmed up for egg sandwiches or as an accompaniment for sausage gravy

2¼ cups all-purpose flour
1 teaspoon kosher salt
1 tablespoon baking powder
1 teaspoon baking soda
5 tablespoons cold unsalted butter
1 cup buttermilk
1 teaspoon salted butter, melted

Preheat oven to 400 degrees Fahrenheit. Line a baking sheet with parchment paper. In a large mixing bowl, sift together the flour, salt, baking powder and baking soda. Using a pastry cutter or two knives, cut the butter into the flour mixture until it forms coarse crumbs. Add the buttermilk and stir to combine until moistened.

Turn the dough out onto a floured board and knead gently for 10 to 15 seconds to bring the dough together. Flatten out and fold over the dough onto itself three or four times. This will create layers.

Dust the board with additional flour and use a rolling pin to roll out the dough to half-inch thickness. Use a three-inch biscuit cutter to cut the biscuits out, re-kneading and rolling the dough as needed.

Brush the tops of the biscuits with melted butter. Slide into the oven and bake for 14 to 16 minutes, until golden.

Cooking tip: Out of buttermilk? No problem. Stir one teaspoon of white vinegar or lemon juice into one cup of milk. Let it sit for ten minutes. Stir and use as directed.

Sausage Gravy
Serves 4
Prep time: 5 minutes
Cook time: 20 minutes

Creamy and comforting, sausage gravy is delightful on an exceptionally cold day served over homemade buttermilk biscuits. And best of all, it's so, so easy to make. Sweet Italian sausage lends this wonderful flavor, but you could use crumbled breakfast sausage too.

1 pound ground sweet Italian sausage
1 small onion, chopped
2 tablespoons all-purpose flour
1½ cups milk
1 tablespoon Worcestershire sauce
1 teaspoon dried rosemary
salt and pepper, to taste
buttermilk biscuits, prepared

Heat a large skillet over medium heat. Add the sausage and onion and cook, stirring frequently, until the sausage is cooked through. Be sure to break apart the sausage as it cooks. Pour off drippings. Add the flour to the skillet and mix well. Cook for 1 minute, stirring. Stir in the milk, Worcestershire sauce and rosemary. Bring to a simmer (it should be steaming hot). Reduce heat to low and simmer for 5 to 8 minutes, or until thickened, stirring frequently. Taste and season with salt and pepper as desired. Serve over warm split biscuits.

Cooking tip: Since this comes together so swiftly, always make the biscuits first.

Good, Basic Biscuit Sandwiches
Serves 4

As the title suggests, these are just good, basic biscuit sandwiches fit for breakfast. The recipe is easily adapted to make as few as one sandwich or as many as you like.

4 buttermilk biscuits, warmed
salted butter, to taste
4 slices American or cheddar cheese
4 large eggs
2 ounces breakfast meat (sausage, ham or bacon), heated or cooked (optional)

Slice the warmed biscuits in half, butter as desired and place one slice of cheese on top of one half. Cook the eggs over easy. Using a nonstick skillet over medium heat. Cook one egg at a time, flipping once, until the whites are set. Place one on top of the cheese on the biscuit halves. Top with the heated (cooked) breakfast meat, if using. Enjoy immediately.

Cooking tip: Don't be afraid to change up the toppings here. This sandwich can also be delicious with a little baby spinach, avocado and/ or tomato on top. Leftover corned beef hash is good too!

Easy Slow Cooker Thanksgiving Turkey Breast
Serves 8 to 10
Prep time: 10 minutes
Cook time: 7 hours

So many diner favorites begin with freshly cooked turkey. This easy method doesn't require you to cook a full turkey or be tethered to the kitchen all day—a win-win since you get to enjoy the fresh turkey.

2 sweet onions, peeled and quartered
1 bone-in turkey breast (about 5–7 pounds), skin removed
2 teaspoons garlic powder
1 teaspoon dried sage
1 teaspoon dried thyme
1 teaspoon salt
½ cup water
cooking oil spray

Arrange the onions in the bottom of the slow cooker and position the turkey, breast side up, on top. In a small bowl, mix together the garlic powder, sage, thyme and salt. Rub all over the turkey. Pour the water into the bottom of the slow cooker. I use a six-quart slow cooker for this. Spray the turkey with cooking oil spray.

Cover and set the slow cooker to low. Cook for 5 to 7 hours, until cooked through. If using a turkey with a pop-out button, watch for the button to pop. Otherwise, use a kitchen thermometer to measure the internal temperature of the turkey. When it reaches 165 degrees Fahrenheit, as measured at the thickest part of the breast, it's fully cooked. Remove from the slow cooker and allow the turkey to rest for 20 minutes before slicing. For best results, tent the turkey with aluminum foil while it's resting.

Cooking tip: This can be made in advance, carved and stored in the fridge for use. You can also freeze portions for later. I highly recommend thinly slicing the turkey.

Homemade Turkey Club
Serves 1 (recipe is easy doubled for more)
Prep time: 10 minutes

3 slices bread (white, wheat or rye)
mayonnaise (optional)
4 slices bacon, cooked until crisp
4 ounces turkey breast (best from a Thanksgiving-style turkey), thinly sliced
4 slices tomatoes (thin)
2 leaves romaine or green leaf lettuce
4 toothpicks with fancy ends

Toast the bread. If using, thinly spread mayonnaise on one side of each slice. Lay one slice of toast, mayonnaise side up, on a cutting board. Top with bacon, turkey, tomato and lettuce. Top with the un-mayonnaised slice of toast. Top with bacon, turkey, tomato and lettuce and then the final slice of bread, mayonnaise side down. Stick four toothpicks in the sandwich. Cut into quarters (one toothpick per quarter).

Cooking tip: If you aren't a fan of mayo, omit it from this recipe. It could be replaced with thinly sliced avocado or just fully omitted. For best results, don't ever, ever use turkey bacon.

Turkey Cottage Pie
Serves 4
Prep time: 15 minutes
Cook time: 45 minutes

Comfort food? Yes, this is definitely that. Hot, freshly made mashed potatoes are best for spreading on this. But if you are using leftover mashed potatoes, drop them on top in by the spoonful.

2 tablespoons olive oil
1 sweet onion, diced
1 cup cubed carrots
½ cup frozen peas
salt and pepper, to taste
1 pound cooked turkey breast, cubed
2 cups leftover turkey gravy
2 cups leftover mashed potatoes
1 tablespoon unsalted butter, melted

Preheat oven to 375 degrees Fahrenheit. In a large skillet, heat the olive oil over medium heat. Add the onions and carrots. Cook, stirring frequently, until softened (about 8 to 10 minutes). Stir in the peas and cook for an additional 2 to 3 minutes until mostly defrosted. In an eight-by-eight-inch glass baking dish, combine the vegetable mixture with the cubed turkey and gravy. Stir well to combine. Spoon the mashed potatoes on top. Brush gently with butter. Bake in the preheated oven for 20 to 30 minutes, until bubbly at the sides.

Cooking tip: Mashed potatoes are delightful on this, but stuffing can be too. If you'd prefer to use stuffing, omit the mashed potatoes and butter. Spoon the stuffing on and bake as directed.

ONE-OFF RECIPES FOR DINER CLASSICS

Of course, some classic recipes are inspired by Maine diner classics.

Blueberry Streusel Muffins
Yields 12
Prep time: 15 minutes
Cook time: 25 minutes

Soft, tender blueberry streusel muffins are perfect for breakfast. The crunchy streusel topping, made with brown sugar, butter and more, makes them special.

Streusel
¼ cup all-purpose flour
⅓ cup packed brown sugar
½ teaspoon ground cinnamon
2 tablespoons unsalted butter, firm

Muffin
¾ cup milk
¼ cup vegetable oil
1 large egg
2 cups all-purpose flour
½ cup sugar
2 teaspoons baking powder
½ teaspoon salt
1 ¼ cups blueberries

Preheat oven to 400 degrees Fahrenheit and line 12 muffin cups with paper liners. In a small bowl, prepare the streusel topping. Sift in the flour, brown sugar and cinnamon and then stir to combine well. Use a pastry blender or two knives crisscrossing to cut the butter into the dry mixture. Continue cutting the butter in until mixture is crumbly. Set bowl aside.

In a large bowl, prepare the muffin batter. Whisk together the milk, oil and egg. Stir in flour, sugar, baking powder and salt. Batter should be moistened and will still be lumpy. Stir in blueberries.

Use a large cookie scoop or a tablespoon to drop batter into the 12 lined muffin cups, dividing equally. Top with about one tablespoon of the streusel topping each. Place the pan into the preheated oven and cook for 20 to 25 minutes, until a toothpick inserted in the center comes out clean. Remove from oven and transfer to a wire cooling rack immediately.

Cooking tip: Blueberries are Maine's state berry, but these muffins are also delicious with raspberries or blackberries.

Blueberry Buttermilk Pancakes
Serves 4 (two pancakes each)
Prep time: 10 minutes
Cook time: 25 minutes

Blueberry pancakes are a staple at many Maine diners. Soft, thick buttermilk pancakes dotted with blueberries are delightful with real Maine maple syrup. Be sure to use wild blueberries, which can be found at Maine farmers markets in the summer and in the freezer section in the winter. Either fresh or frozen will work.

1 large egg
1 cup all-purpose flour
1 cup buttermilk
1 tablespoon sugar
2 tablespoons canola oil
1 teaspoon vanilla extract
1 teaspoon baking powder
1 teaspoon baking soda
½ teaspoon kosher salt
1 cup wild Maine blueberries, fresh or frozen (if using frozen, do not defrost)
1 teaspoon unsalted butter

Preheat a griddle (a large one if you have it) on the stove over heat set to just below its medium setting. In a stand mixer fitted with the whisk attachment, beat the egg until light yellow and frothy—about 2 minutes. Add the flour, buttermilk, sugar, oil, vanilla extract, baking powder, baking soda and salt to the mixer. Beat on low until just combined. Fold the blueberries into the batter.

Melt the butter all over the griddle. Drop the batter in rounds (I usually do about ¼ cup of batter per pancake) on the hot griddle and cook. When the pancake bubbles all over, it's time to flip. Cook until golden brown on both sides. Serve with real Maine maple syrup.

Cooking tip: My favorite way to keep pancakes warm while cooking others is to place them inside my Dutch oven. They remain warm and soft. You can also turn on the oven to 200 degrees and store them on a baking sheet in there. They tend to be less soft when you do so.

Stuffed Basil, Ham and Cheese Omelet with Tomatoes
Serves 1
Prep time: 5 minutes
Cook time: 10 minutes

Inspired by the stuffed omelets available at diners across the state, including Becky's Diner in Portland, this easy omelet is filled with ham, cheese, basil and tomatoes. It's delightful. Serve with buttered toast.

1 egg
2 tablespoons milk
2 basil leaves, shredded
½ cup diced ham
½ cup cheddar or Swiss cheese, shredded
¼ cup tomatoes, diced

Combine egg, milk and basil in a small bowl and beat until the egg is frothy. Season with a little salt and pepper (just a little) and whisk to combine. Spray a small skillet with cooking spray and place on a burner over medium heat. When the pan is heated, pour in the egg mixture. Cook until the omelet is almost completely cooked through. Spread the ham, cheese and tomato on one half of the omelet and fold the other half over. Continue cooking for 2 to 3 minutes, until cheese begins to melt.

Cooking tip: Feel free to change up the fillings in this omelet. This is also good with sausage or different cheeses. You could even make a vegetable version.

Easy Creamy Macaroni and Cheese
Serves 4
Prep time: 5 minutes
Cook time: 20 minutes

Creamy and flavorful, this easy macaroni and cheese recipe is better than the box. Whatever you do, do not omit the dry mustard—it's a key ingredient for enhancing the flavor of the cheddar cheese.

½ pound macaroni pasta (or small shells)
1 tablespoon unsalted butter
1 tablespoon all-purpose flour
1 cup milk
1 cup shredded sharp cheddar cheese
¼ teaspoon dry ground mustard
kosher salt, to taste

Fill a pot with water and set it on a burner on high heat. Bring to a boil and add the pasta. Stir and reduce heat to medium.

Melt the butter in a small saucepan over medium heat. Once it's completely melted, add the flour. Whisk well to combine, using a rubber spatula or a spoon to scrape the sides as needed. Continue, whisking constantly, until the flour is fully combined with the butter and turns a light amber color. Whisk in the milk and continue whisking until the roux (flour/butter mixture) is fully incorporated. Continue cooking, whisking two or three times, for 2 minutes.

Add the cheddar cheese and dry ground mustard. Whisk well to combine. Remove the pan from the burner. Taste the sauce and season, as necessary, with salt. By now, the pasta should be done cooking (be sure to drain it immediately to keep it al dente). Pour the cheese sauce over the pasta and stir well to combine. Let sit for 5 minutes. Stir again and serve immediately.

Cooking tip: For best results, always grate your own cheddar cheese. Bagged cheeses that come in shreds are mixed with additives that prevent the shreds from sticking together. Those additives will make the sauce taste gritty.

Slow Cooker Beef Stew
Serves four

The lingering scent of slow-cooking beef mixed with red wine and garlic is mouthwatering to come home to. This recipe is an easy way to let stew cook low and slow to perfection. Serve it with biscuits.

1 ½ pounds beef stew meat
4 cups beef broth or stock
1 cup red wine
½ pound carrots, peeled and cut into one-inch chunks
1 pound Idaho potatoes, rinsed and cut into one-inch chunks
½ pound sweet potatoes, rinsed and cut into one-inch chunks
4 cloves garlic minced
8–10 sprigs fresh thyme
salt and pepper, to taste

Combine all ingredients, except the salt and pepper, in a slow cooker and stir well. Set the slow cooker to low and cook for ten to twelve hours. The stew is done when the vegetables are tender and the meat is falling apart. Remove the sprigs of thyme (for easier removal, tie them together with kitchen string before cooking). Season with salt and pepper to taste and thicken, if desired. A little cornstarch whisked into broth and added to the stew about fifteen minutes before you want to serve will thicken it slightly.

Cooking tip: If you don't wish to cook with red wine, add extra broth or stock and one tablespoon of Worcestershire sauce.

American Chop Suey
Serves 4 to 6
Prep time: 10 minutes
Cook time: 20 minutes

This is a New England classic that has been served at many family tables for decades. Everyone seems to make it a little differently—and there's definitely room for personalization here.

1 tablespoon olive oil
1 small yellow onion, diced
1 green bell pepper, diced
2 cloves garlic, minced
salt and pepper, to taste
1 pound ground beef
2 tablespoons fresh Italian herbs, finely chopped
1 jar marinara sauce
1 pound penne pasta, cooked

Heat olive oil in a large skillet. Add onion, green bell pepper and garlic. Cover and cook, stirring occasionally, until the vegetables are softened—about 10 minutes. Uncover and season with salt and pepper.

Push the veggies to one side of the skillet and add the ground beef. Brown, stirring and breaking apart as it cooks. When the beef is fully browned and crumbled, combine with veggies. Carefully pour excess fat into a bowl (you'll want to discard that later). Add the Italian herbs and stir well to combine.

Pour the sauce into the skillet and toss well. Add the pasta, toss again and let cook for 2 to 3 minutes until warmed throughout.

Cooking tip: This can be made with other pasta shapes too. Try it with elbow macaroni or rotini if you prefer.

Barbecue Turkey Bacon Meatloaf
Serves 6
Prep time: 15 minutes
Cook time: 55 minutes

My grandmother used to make meatloaf with ground beef, onions, seasonings and a slathering of tomato paste. It wasn't my favorite dish she made. But over the years, I've discovered that a wilder version of meatloaf is more my speed. This one combines ground turkey with veggies, bacon and seasonings, and it's coated in barbecue sauce—a delight.

olive oil or cooking spray
1 pound ground turkey
6 slices bacon, chopped
¾ cup diced onions
¾ cup red bell diced pepper
¾ cup oats
3 tablespoons Worcestershire sauce
3 tablespoons barbecue sauce, plus ¼ cup, divided
2 teaspoons kosher salt
1 teaspoon ground black pepper

Preheat the oven to 350 degrees Fahrenheit. Line a baking sheet with aluminum foil and brush with oil (or spray with cooking oil spray). Set aside.

In a large bowl, stir together the ground turkey, chopped bacon, onions, red bell pepper, oats, Worcestershire sauce, three tablespoons of barbecue sauce and salt and pepper until it's really well mixed. You want all the flavors evenly distributed throughout.

Turn the mixture out onto the prepared baking sheet and use your hands to press it into a loaf form, about one-inch thick. Bake for 45 to 50 minutes, until well browned on the outside. Brush the meatloaf with the remaining fourth cup of barbecue sauce. Return to the oven and bake for an additional 5 minutes. Let cool slightly before slicing and serving.

Cooking tip: Turkey bacon can be substituted for the pork bacon that this recipe calls for. Be sure to choose a barbecue sauce that you like the flavor of.

Individual Lobster Pies for Two
Serves 2
Prep time: 10 minutes
Cook time: 35 minutes

Sweet lobster is enrobed in a lovely garlic butter and then baked to perfection with a buttery, crunchy, sherry-infused topping. A squeeze of lemon gives a beautiful acid counterpoint to this decadent dish. This is something to make and share with someone special.

4 tablespoons unsalted butter, divided
1 clove garlic, minced
½ pound cooked lobster meat (about two 1-pound lobsters steamed and meat removed from shells)
½ teaspoon paprika
1 tablespoon dry sherry
½ cup panko

Preheat oven to 375 degrees Fahrenheit. Melt 1 tablespoon of butter in a small skillet. Add the garlic and cook for 1 to 2 minutes until fragrant. Remove from heat and add the lobster. Toss well. Season with paprika, salt and pepper. Stir well.

Divide the lobster evenly between two large ramekins or single-serving oven-safe baking dishes (they should hold one to one and a half cups of food).

In a small saucepan, melt the remaining three tablespoons of butter. Stir in the sherry and let cook, stirring, for about 1 minute, until bubbly. Stir in the panko. Remove from the stove and spoon the mixture over the lobster. Bake in the preheated oven for 20 to 25 minutes, until golden brown. Serve with lemon wedges.

Cooking tip: The most cost-effective way to make this dish is to start with whole lobsters. If you are purchasing from a fish market, often they will steam your lobsters for free.

Maine Diner Trivia

Across the Pine Tree State, diners serve as hubs of community life while welcoming folks from all over. And many have storied histories going back decades. Test your knowledge of Maine diners. Can you name each diner here? Check your answers at the end.

1. This diner was once called the Norwago Diner. Rumor has it the owner couldn't afford the cost of re-lettering the diner, so it simply changed from Norway Diner to Norwago Diner.

2. This dining car company built only a handful of diners when it operated in the 1920s.

3. When the current owner of this classic Maine diner decided to buy it, he had to purchase from a unique source: the City of Portland.

4. This Pollard diner has been moved once since it arrived in Maine—essentially from one end of a parking lot to another, though it was actually moved to make room for that parking lot.

5. Built by the Worcester Lunch Car Company in the 1920s, this Maine diner still has its original sliding wooden door as an entrance.

6. Famous among locals and tourists alike for its lobster pie, when this diner first opened, it was closed during tourist season.

7. Originally a lunch cart, this iconic diner has grown piece by piece with more than a dozen additions.

8. Three diners from this Massachusetts lunch car company remain in operation in Maine today.

9. Uniquely located on a bridge, this diner still bears its original name on the side, Heald's.

10. This relatively new diner was opened by the person who owns several dining cars not presently in operation.

11. This Maine diner is housed in a shiny prefabricated building created by a Florida company that also built the structures that house two Denny's locations in Maine.

12. When this diner opened in 1991, it catered to a hungry wharf crowd. It still does, but it also attracts tourists and the attention of major food media.

13. Located in Eastport in Washington County, the name of this diner is actually the combination of the original owners' names.

14. Pat's Diner opened in Gardiner, Maine, in 1965. What was the make and model of the diner building?

15. Formally called an ice cream parlor, this Maine diner changed its name after it began holding popular cruise nights.

Answers

1. Brunswick Diner; 2. The Pollard Company; 3. Miss Portland Diner; 4. Palace Diner; 5. Deluxe Diner; 6. Maine Diner; 7. Moody's Diner; 8. Worchester Lunch Car Company; 9. A1 Diner; 10. Farmington D; 11. Blast from the Past; 12. Becky's Diner; 13. WaCo Diner; 14. Valentine Diners Double Deluxe; 15. Nicky's Cruisin' Diner

Recommended Reading

Garbin, Randy. *Diners of New England*. Mechanicsburg, PA: Stackpole Books, 2005.
This history of diners throughout New England has interesting information about diners in each state, along with the make of many of the prefabricated buildings. Written in 2005, it's particularly interesting to read about diners that have closed in the last dozen years or so.

Genthner, Nancy Moody, and Kerry Leichtman. *What's Cooking at Moody's Diner*. West Rockport, ME: Dancing Bear Books, 2003.
A collection of family history, diner history and remembrances by the Moodys—plus, diner recipes.

Maine Courses. Wells, ME: Maine Diner, 1996.
This is a cookbook with a little bit of history woven in. It is a good book for those with the Maine Diner as part of their personal history.

Rolph, Sarah. *A1 Diner*. Gardiner, ME: Tilbury House, 2006.
History and recipes meet in this lovely ode to the A1 Diner. It features stories and favorite diner recipes from past owners, along with historic photos through the early 2000s.

Urban, Mike. *The New England Diner Cookbook*. Woodstock: VT: Countryman Press, 2014.
For those wanting to enjoy more Maine diner classics at home, this cookbook offers recipes for the quintessential American diner cuisine. It also includes some history of notable diners.

Index

About the Author

Gabor Degre for The Bangor Daily News.

S arah Walker Caron is an award-winning food writer, columnist and author based in Maine. She's been writing about food since before Pinterest, Twitter or Instagram existed.

The author of six books, including *The Super Easy 5-Ingredient Cookbook* and *One-Pot Pasta*, Sarah believes that good food is for everyone and that anyone can learn to make it. But as much as she loves cooking, she also adores restaurants—particularly ones where she can find a good plate of corned beef hash and lovely fluffy pancakes.

By day, she's the senior editor, features, for the *Bangor Daily News* and the editor of *Bangor Metro* and hellohomestead.com. She writes the In Season Now column for *Bangor Metro* magazine and Farm to Kitchen Table, a weekly food column, for the *Bangor Daily News*. By night, she's the blogger voice behind Sarah's Cucina Bella (www.sarahscucinabella.com), a fourteen-plus-year-old food blog focusing on quick and easy from-scratch recipes for busy people, as well as food travel and good books.

Caron teaches journalism at the University of Maine and blogging at Husson University. She lives in the Bangor area with her two kids and her friendly black cat named Bippity.

Visit us at
www.historypress.com
··